Grand Canyon - Flagstaff

STAGE
COACH
LINE

A History
& Exploration
Guide

by Richard and Sherry Mangum

Hexagon Press, Inc.
Flagstaff Arizona
1999

Acknowledgements

Our thanks for their help in the preparation of this book go to:

Dan and Diane Cassidy of Five Quail Books, Phoenix; Roger Hartman, owner of Lake Mary Stables, Flagstaff; the crew at the Grand Canyon Museum Archives and Library: Carolyn Richard, Colleen Hyde, Kim Besom, Michael Quinn, and Sarah Stebbins; members of the staff at the Museum of Northern Arizona: Michael Fox, Tony Marinella, and Michael O'Hara; Steve Verkamp; Joe Meehan of the Arizona Historical Society's Pioneer Museum at Flagstaff; Teri Cleeland and Larry Lesko of the Kaibab Forest Service; Peter Pilles and Gallina Franz, of the Coconino Forest Service; Scott Thybony; Shelley Silbert and Bob Jensen of the Nature Conservancy, and Dr. John Hildebrand.

Cover photo, *Grand Canyon From Mather Point,* by Sherry G. Mangum

Historic photo of stage from *Arizona Sketches* by J. A. Munk

Cover design by Joan Carstensen of Sullivan/Santamaria Designs, Flagstaff

Produced by Northland Graphics, Flagstaff

Hexagon Press, Inc.

300 E. Bennett Drive

Flagstaff, AZ 86001

e-mail: mangum@hexagonpress.com

Table of Contents

The Authors

RICHARD K. MANGUM is a native of Flagstaff. From childhood he has enjoyed getting out into the country surrounding his home and exploring the area.

After graduation from Flagstaff High School in 1954, he attended the University of Arizona, where he earned a B.A. in English and a J. D. in Law. He practiced law in Flagstaff from 1961-1976; then was a Superior Court Judge, until he retired in 1993.

He is presently engaged full-time in writing, exploring and studying—having the time of his life. He is a Historian-in-Residence at the Museum of Northern Arizona, and a member of numerous professional organizations

SHERRY G. MANGUM has lived in Flagstaff since she was seven, and remembers always enjoying the outdoors.

Inheriting a love of photography from her parents, both professionals, she has refined her skills to produce her landscapes that have been widely used in publications.

Her work is recognized as exceptionally good at capturing the lighting and spirit of her beloved Colorado Plateau and she has been published locally, nationally and internationally since 1978.

She and her husband conduct historic walks through Flagstaff's downtown district wearing costumes that Sherry designs and sews. She is also a historian-in-residencc at the Museum of Northern Arizona.

Preface

The Grand Canyon-Flagstaff Stagecoach Line operated from May 1892 until the close of the tourist season in 1900, a span of some nine years, and in so doing, entered into the legends of the West. There were other stage lines to Grand Canyon at the time, running from Williams, Ash Fork and Peach Springs, but only the Flagstaff had the blessing, sponsorship and support of the railroad, making it the "official" Grand Canyon stage line. It was a boon to Flagstaff's economy, making it the Gateway to the Grand Canyon.

At the end of its life, the stage line succumbed to two powerful competitors that were to doom horse-drawn transportation altogether, the railroad and the automobile But while it lasted, the stagecoach was king. Riding the coach and roughing it at the Canyon were unforgettable experiences, prompting one travel writer who took the trip in 1897 to express the opinion of many, "If ever a stage road should survive, to bring memories of the merry coaching days of old, it is this line between Flagstaff and the Grand Canyon."

When we began this project, we thought that we had plenty of material for the book, but as we dug into it, we found that we not only had to find new material, but to "unlearn" much of what we thought we knew. It turned out that the first modern author to write about the line filled his work with error and surmise. His statements were copied unthinkingly by those who followed, coalescing into a body of knowledge that was fatally flawed.

Most people who feel that they know something about the stagecoach line would parrot these "facts": the terminus was the Bank Hotel; the first stop was the Dillman Ranch, where Mrs. Dillman sold Teddy Roosevelt a refreshment and kept the silver dollar he gave her as a souvenir; that the line ran only on Monday, Wednesday and Friday to the Canyon, returning to Flagstaff on Tuesday, Thursday and Saturday; that it ran to the Grandview Hotel at the Canyon; that the passengers got out and pushed the coach up steep grades; that the coach ran up Lockwood Canyon in bad weather; that its life ended late in 1901 when the first train ran from Williams to the Grand Canyon. We learned that all of these "facts" are wholly or partially in error, and are pleased to set the record straight. As hard as we have tried to be accurate, we apologize for any errors of our own.

We have written other historical books, *Flagstaff Historic Walk* and *Flagstaff Album*, in addition to scores of magazine articles, and consider ourselves to be historians. We have also written recreation guides to northern Arizona, *Flagstaff Hikes, Sedona Hikes* and *The Williams Guidebook*. We were able to combine our knowledge of history and of the roads and pathways of the area in writing this book, and the effort has been a joy.

We have covered every inch of the ground, which was often difficult because of scanty information. Finally we amassed enough knowledge, maps and field work to feel that we could speak authoritatively about the subject. It became obvious early that the Western Route was fairly well known but that the Eastern Route had become neglected and lost to memory. We have relocated it now and have enjoyed our many hours among the cinder hills prowling and exploring in doing so.

Grand Canyon tourism is still an important part of Flagstaff's economy. We hope you will enjoy the story of the enterprise that got it all started.

Painting by F. H. Lungren for the Santa Fe

History of the Town of Flagstaff [1]

The Anglo settlement of the area now known as the City of Flagstaff occurred in 1876. Early that year a handful of sheep ranchers from California came into the territory to escape a drought that had lasted for several years on the Coast. They had passed through northern Arizona on their way to California years earlier and remembered the virgin grasslands around the San Francisco Peaks they had seen in passage. One of these men, Thomas F. McMillan, located a homestead just north of the present town, and used a nearby spring to water his flocks.

In July 1876, a group of young men, later called the Second Boston Party, passed through the district. They knew that the Fourth of July would fall during their travels and were ready for it, carrying a flag so they could celebrate the nation's Centennial. On the evening of July 3, 1876, they received permission from McMillan to camp at his water hole, at Antelope Spring. Next morning they held a ceremony, stripping a pine tree of its branches and hanging Old Glory from its top. When they moved on, they took their flag with them but left the tree, the flag staff, in place. It was used as a landmark thereafter, and travelers were told that if they were in the vicinity of the Peaks and needed a place with water at which to camp, they should look for the flag staff. Soon the place was informally called Flagstaff and appeared on a government survey map with that name in 1878.

In 1880, the Atlantic & Pacific Railroad began building its line west from Albuquerque, bound for California. A group of railroad surveyors entered the Flagstaff area and set up camp near Old Town Spring, next to the railroad right-of-way, in April 1880. In time they were joined by other construction workers: graders, tie choppers, etc., and a large construction camp sprang up at the site. Entrepreneurs, learning that the camp existed,

Old Town Flagstaff 1883

New Town Flagstaff 1883

Early travelers to the Grand Canyon had to camp en route

Grand Cañon of Arizona

John Hance, pioneer Grand Canyon guide

set up businesses catering to the needs of the railroad workers and a little community became established. By 1881 the hamlet had enough population to qualify for a post office. This meant that the community had to have a name, so a citizens' meeting was held. Several names were proposed and debated, but finally a consensus was reached: the place would be called Flagstaff.

On August 1, 1882, the tracks reached Flagstaff, and railroad officials discovered that it was a robust little community, much more than the temporary construction camp they had anticipated finding. Trains had to stop at Old Town Spring for water, so Atlantic & Pacific officials decided to take advantage of the situation and install a depot and yards at Flagstaff, though it had never been their original intention to establish a town there. The location of the settlement at the spring was on a slope, which made it difficult for westbound trains to get into motion after stopping for water; so the railroad built its depot on a tract of flat land it owned about a mile to the east in the late summer of 1882.

By the summer of 1883 it seemed to some of the business owners that they would have more trade if they relocated to be near the depot rather than staying at the spring; so a few of them moved. The first two men to relocate, in the summer of 1883, were P. J. Brannen with his general store, and Charles Hickerson with his saloon. Others followed, and for a while there were two Flagstaffs: the original site, which was called the West End or Old Town; and the East End or New Town. The advantage went to New Town, which quickly began to outstrip Old Town. In 1884 a fire devastated Old Town and the owners of its destroyed commercial buildings did not bother to reconstruct their burnt-out structures, moving to New Town instead. From that time there was no longer any question about the location of Flagstaff: it was centered on the depot.

Early Tourism

From the time the first settlers entered into the Flagstaff area, they explored it to find out what resources it contained and soon discovered that they were sitting in the middle of a natural treasure house of scenic wonders, the greatest of which was the Grand Canyon, some seventy miles to the north.

Reaching the Canyon was difficult in the early days. There were no roads from Flagstaff to the Grand Canyon at first, and explorers had to navigate their way by rough reckoning; so it was seen by few, even though its fame was told to many. Between Flagstaff and the Grand Canyon were good grasslands, and a number of early settlers established sheep ranches on the range, which was open to homestead entry. Among the earliest of these ranchers were the men of the Hull family, Philip, Philip Jr. and William, who located adjacent 160-acre homestead tracts at a place later known as East Cedar Ranch, perhaps as early as 1880. To get to their ranch, they traveled the existing Flagstaff-Tuba City road to a point north of the San Francisco Peaks then branched off with a new wagon road that they extended to their ranches.[2]

Since there was plenty of land and few settlers, many of the first homesteaders put down stakes on a likely piece of land but continued to look around for greener pastures. They were free to do so, having squatter's rights to protect them while they searched. Philip Hull Jr., while roaming the region, visited the Grand Canyon in the Grandview area in February 1880.[3] He found some good pasturage that might be favorable for sheep ranching, except for one thing: there was no water. He explored further and found a water source about a mile south of the Rim, where the Hulls established another ranch site about thirty miles north of their original spread. They established a winter quarters for their sheep ranch there, developing

The Ayer lumber mill, Flagstaff's first smokestack industry

E. E. Ayer, Flagstaff lumber king. First tourist

Sharlot Hall Museum 1703-P

John Hance, on horse, at his tourist camp. He lived
in the cabin. His guests stayed in tents.

water tanks and building a cabin. This Canyon-area ranch was in operation at least as early as 1883. The Hulls hired John Hance to work for them as a ranch hand.[4] Hance was interested in locating minerals and explored the Canyon to see what he could find, using an old Indian trail, which he improved, to give him access to the Inner Gorge.[5]

At this time, the land around the Grand Canyon was ordinary federal domain with no special status. It was open to homesteading, mining, lumbering, grazing and any other use. It had never been surveyed, so there were very few identified holdings, only a few squatters' claims such as those of Hance and the Hulls. The settlers simply helped themselves. "Everything is free as air,"[6] the newspaper reported.[7] The early settlers laid out trails and used the land however they chose. Hance took possession of a strategic spot for his homestead: it was just a few yards from the Rim, it was at the terminus of the Flagstaff wagon road, and it was very near the trailhead for the Old Hance Trail.

The arrival of the railroad in Flagstaff in the summer of 1882 opened the area to tourism, allowing travelers a convenient and comfortable way to reach the formerly remote Arizona town by train. The Hull brothers conducted the first known tour of the Grand Canyon in February 1884 when William Hull took Flagstaff lumber magnate E. E. Ayer to the Canyon, where John Hance acted as his guide, taking him down his trail.[8] (This path became known as the Old Hance Trail.)[9] Hance enjoyed the experience, perhaps picked up a nice tip, and decided that there was a future in tourism. About June 15, 1884, he homesteaded a 160-acre tract of land adjacent to the rim where Glendale Spring was located and built a cabin there, less than a mile north of the Hull ranch, intending to use it as a headquarters for tourism.[10]

In Flagstaff, the editor of its newspaper, the *Arizona Champion*, probably stimulated by the Ayer trip, opined in May 1884 that a road to the Grand Canyon was needed.[11] Action was taken on the suggestion, and two roads were developed in the summer of 1884, which we call the Eastern Route and the Western Route, based on whether they went around the San Francisco Peaks on the east or west side. The first action on the Eastern Route was taken by Jim Black and J. W. Spafford, who scouted the way in June 1884.[12] A wagon road along the route they selected seemed feasible, so Jim Black and some of his brothers followed up soon with a survey.[13] In December 1884 the Black brothers took a party of Atlantic & Pacific Railroad officials over their proposed route. The *Champion* reported that the reaction of the officials was positive: "It would seem that the A & P

Ad for freelance service to Grand Canyon

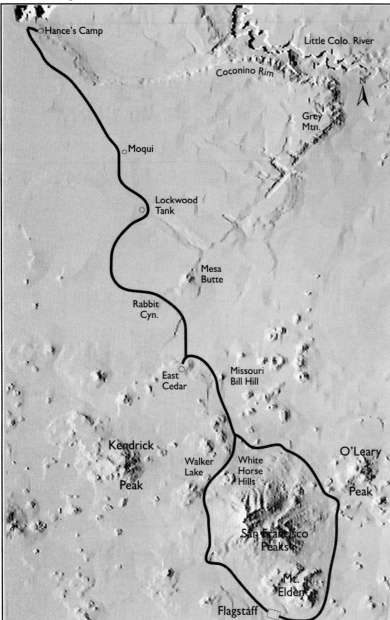

company were going to take hold of the new route, and next summer we expect to see a road made and all the excursionists go to that popular place of resort from this place."[14]

In June 1884, William Hull, John Hance and Silas Ruggles built the Western Route.[15] It already existed from Flagstaff to the Hull Ranch at East Cedar and needed only to be extended from there about thirty-five miles to the Rim.

Clearly 1884 was a pivotal year in the establishment of Grand Canyon tourism. It saw a well-publicized visit by a notable, wealthy gentleman, which was important because the knowledge would invite other wealthy people to make the trip, which had theretofore been considered only the province of hardened pioneers. The year also saw the building of the Western Route, construction under way on the Eastern Route, and the establishment of a tourist base with guides at the Canyon.

This relief map shows the Eastern and Western routes. By studying the map, one can see how the pathfinders negotiated the numerous hills and other obstacles. The roads converge north of the San Francisco Peaks. The Grand Canyon makes a big dip to the south at Hance's Camp; so Hance was strategically situation. He had water, a scenic location at a particularly beautiful part of the Canyon, and his camp was at the end of the shortest line between Flagstaff and Grand Canyon .

The First Stage Trips

In 1885 the Hulls and Hance entered into a joint venture for the purpose of taking tourists to the Grand Canyon. Fixing up a farm wagon, they advertised in Flagstaff that they would make excursions to the Canyon for $20 a person, meals not included. They made a trip only when they had enough passengers to fill the wagon.[16] The Hull-Hance operation may not have been the first Grand Canyon tourism operation running from Flagstaff. By the unexpected means of an obituary, the authors have a tantalizing report of another stage line to the Canyon from Flagstaff: in 1937, when J. R. Treat died, the *Coconino Sun* reported that, "At one time Mr. Treat with his brother-in-law, James Lamport, operated the first commercial stage between Flagstaff and Grand Canyon. Mr. Lamport is a brother of Mrs. C. A. Greenlaw."[17] No other information about the Treat-Lamport line has been found. One modern writer mentions a private Flagstaff to Grand Canyon stage line of the early era without identifying the operators.[18] There is another tantalizing reference, which in its entirety reads, "In 1883-84 an attempt was made to establish a stage line from here to the Grand Canyon."[19] In 1885 another Grand Canyon stage line was started, this one by W. W. Bass. However, the line took travelers from the train at Williams and delivered them to Bass Camp, some twenty-five miles west of today's Village.[20]

Mrs. E. E. Ayer. First female tourist

In February 1885 the editor of the *Champion* traveled to the Canyon via the Eastern Route, the one laid out by the Black brothers. He wrote a positive account of his trip, mentioning stops at the ranch of Philip Hull Jr., where he found a spring; Red Horse, beside an ancient Moqui trail, where there was also a spring; and finally Glendale Spring at the Rim.[21] Two weeks later the paper reported that "quite a large number of people" were preparing to go to Grand Canyon via the new [Eastern] route.[22] It is not clear when the Eastern Route progressed from the proposed route seen by Atlantic & Pacific officials in December 1884 to the actual road traveled by the newspaper editor in February 1885, but the road building must have occurred in December 1884 and January 1885. Probably the editor took his February trip to check out the newly finished track.

It must be borne in mind that road building in those days was a rather primitive affair. The land through which these roads had to travel was mostly public domain, so there was no bother about securing permits and rights-of-way; road builders simply helped themselves and followed the best natural course. They did not make cuts or fills or build bridges, but followed the topography, taking the line of least resistance, using simple tools. Road building was mostly a matter of finding a decent path with gentle grades, places to ford streams and gullies, a firm natural roadbed, and water. Horses pulling a vehicle needed water every twenty miles. The road builder might roll some rocks aside and cut off overhanging branches that interfered with passage, but little else would have been done.

In May 1885 E. E. Ayer took another trip to the Canyon, and made another first: he took his wife along. Mrs. Ayer was credited with being the first white woman to reach the bottom of the Canyon.[23] Hiking down the Old Hance Trail as she did was difficult work and required negotiating six dry waterfalls by means of ropes.[24] The indomitable Mrs. Ayer made it all the way to the river, and Ayer Point was named in her honor. The news covering this event opened the tourism door further, showing the world that women might take pleasure in the trip as well as men. Ayer enjoyed his second trip so much that he took another in November 1885.[25] The editor of the *Champion* also went back to the Canyon in November, at the end of the tourist season, and reported that, "The road is in capital condition."[26]

These early trips were taken by means of a single team of horses pulling a buckboard or wagon. If travelers arrived in Flagstaff by train, they would rent the animals, wagons, camping gear and guides necessary to make the

En route to the Canyon in the pre-stage coach era

MNA MS 26-32a

Hull Cabin, about a mile south of Hance's

MNA MS 196-74-1996

The tank at Hull Cabin

trip. Flagstaff livery stable operators reached out for some of the tourist business and began to advertise trips to the Grand Canyon. E. S. Wilcox named his business the Grand Canyon Stables. His large barn stood two doors south of today's Weatherford Hotel on Leroux Street, with his corrals reaching west across the block to Beaver Street. Wilcox did not run a regular stage line to the Canyon; he simply had rigs, tack, camping equipment and a guide ready for hire.

A vehicle drawn by a single team could only travel at about four miles per hour and cover perhaps thirty-five miles in a day, meaning that Flagstaff to Grand Canyon travelers had to spend at least one night on the road, camping out under the stars or in tents, packing bedrolls and camping equipment for the purpose. In spite of these hardships and difficulties, enough people in the 1880s were taking trips to the Canyon so that the potential of tourism could be seen.

By 1886, travel to Grand Canyon was brisk. The editor of the *Arizona Champion* editorialized that the Grand Canyon should be made a National Park.[27] Later he informed his readers that the Pullman Company was going to build a big hotel at the Canyon.[28] John Hance began to advertise himself as a Grand Canyon guide.[29] He also created a small tourist camp of tents around his log cabin at his homestead, which came to be called Hance's Camp.[30]

Since railroads were the dominant investment opportunity of the time, it was inevitable that—with tourism to Grand Canyon from Flagstaff firmly established—there should be a movement to build a railroad to the Canyon. In December 1886, the Flagstaff-Grand Canyon Railroad Company was organized, with several influential Flagstaff men at the helm. The cost of building such a line exceeded the abilities of this local group, so its organizers hired engineers to survey and map a route to show that the railroad was feasible, then wooed several Eastern capitalists.[31] In spite of their efforts they were unable to persuade the Easterners to invest the considerable sums of money necessary to build such a line. For many years thereafter, rumors of a railroad from Flagstaff to the Grand Canyon waxed and waned.[32]

By 1888 travel from Flagstaff to the Grand Canyon was so lively that some major interests began to take a close look at Canyon tourism, the Atlantic & Pacific Railroad for one. From the time that the Atlantic & Pacific was completed to California in 1883, it had experienced trouble with the run across northern Arizona. The area was sparsely populated and except for livestock and lumber there was almost nothing to ship into or out of the region. The idea of persuading tourists to take the line for no other reason than to see the sights along the way was enticing, and—since passenger rates were much higher than freight rates—held out the promise of profit.[33] The railroad realized that heavy advertising would be necessary to tell the ignorant world of the splendors of the area, and that words alone were inadequate to describe the scenery. In 1888 the railroad hired a painter to visit the Canyon and produce art that could be used on calendars, brochures and other media. The Pullman Company, maker of railroad cars, also sent painters to the Canyon. This 1888 effort began a tradition of Grand Canyon railroad advertising art that was to continue for decades, producing galleries of colorful material.[34]

The authors believe that Hance and the Hulls dissolved their partnership in September 1886, the date when Hance began advertising as a Grand Canyon guide. The author of an article written for the Prescott *Journal Miner*, in 1888 (quoted in the *Arizona Champion*) implied that Hance and the Hulls were running separate operations:

> Owing to the long distance necessary to travel from the railroad to reach [the Canyon]—seventy five miles—there are comparatively few people who care to make the trip even to see this wonder of all wonders, and as a consequence the accommodation provided for sight-seers is rather poor, but parties who have recently

returned from there report considerable improvement in progress now.... [The Hull Ranch] is situated about a mile and a half east [sic it was really about a mile south] of Mr. Hance's place, the terminus of the wagon road to the canyon, and consists of a huge reservoir, excavated and constructed by Philip Hull, Jr., and his brothers, at an expense of about $1,600; it covers about sixty square rods and averages fourteen feet in depth.....The Hull boys constructed it to water their sheep from, as this is their winter headquarters. Some day they hope to see a railroad and hotel out there, and say that they have piloted several eastern capitalists at different times along the canyon, and that all talked railroad and hotel very strongly. They say that two different artists have made paintings of this section of the canyon, each 10 x 14 feet, one being sent out by the Pullman Car Co....[35]

Notable in the above article is the observation that Hance's place was the terminus of the wagon road to the canyon; tourists had to make a bit of a detour to get to the Hull Ranch. Although some travelers stopped over at the Hulls' place, Hance had the advantage of being much closer to the Rim and could offer water and pasturage. Besides, he was a colorful character, and his reputation grew to the point that tourists felt that seeing him was an essential part of the Canyon experience. Buckey O'Neill summed up the thoughts of many tourists when he wrote, "God made the cañon, John Hance the trails. Without the other, neither would be complete."[36]

In the late 1880s the Hulls began to divest themselves of their East Cedar Ranch property and concentrate on their Grand Canyon lands.[37] Just as they were getting their tourist operation into full swing, Philip Hull Jr. died in 1888, at the age of forty-one, no doubt taking the steam out of the family's operation, though William continued to run the tourism business for a while and may have continued to provide a stagecoach to the Canyon until 1892.[38] Philip Hull Sr. sold his interest in the East Cedar Ranch to the Arizona Cattle Company in 1889.[39]

By 1889, the Atlantic & Pacific Railroad began to advertise excursions to Grand Canyon from Flagstaff in its timetable, though these trips were conducted by independent operators unaffiliated with the railroad.[40] Much interest in the Grand Canyon was created in 1889 by the Stanton Expedition, which ran the Colorado River, surveying for a railroad line to run along the bottom of the Grand Canyon, on the banks of the river.[41] John Hance continued to advertise his services as a Grand Canyon guide.[42]

In 1890, the *Champion* reported, "A stage line to the Grand Canyon has been started. The first stage will leave next Monday morning at 9:00 o'clock from the Bank Hotel."[43] No other information is available, and no follow-up reporting about the line could be found. Many of the 1890 newspapers are missing from the archives, leaving a frustrating gap in the history of this period.

Stimulated by the excitement created by the Stanton Expedition[44], the Cameron brothers, Ralph and Niles, and Pete Berry went from Flagstaff to the Grand Canyon in 1890 to prospect for valuable minerals. At first they used the Old Hance Trail to go into the Canyon to the Tonto Platform, traversing the Canyon on the Tonto. Soon afterwards, they found an old Indian trail some twenty miles to the west and spent weeks improving it to give themselves access to the inner canyon without paying tribute to Hance. They called this new trail the Bright Angel Trail.[45] Others were also actively prospecting at the Canyon at this time.

Tourism from Flagstaff to Grand Canyon no doubt continued in 1890, but no direct accounts of activity have been found from available records.

In 1891 Flagstaff livery stable owner A. C. Morse raised two hundred dollars from Flagstaff businessmen, supplemented the sum with three hundred dollars of his own and hired a group of men to improve the road to the Grand Canyon.[46] Soon afterwards it was reported that he was fitting up his big coach to take a group of fifteen to the Canyon.[47]

NAU–PH.83

Prospectors pose in Flagstaff before leaving for the Grand Canyon

Land of Sunshine, by Tinker

Ad run by A. C. Morse for his livery stable, 1887

Grand Cañon of the Colorado

Hance Camp. The appearance has been improved, but it is still very rustic

MNA MS 196-74-1999

Buckboard on way to Canyon, north of Flagstaff

West of Flagstaff, William Bass began building his stagecoach road from Williams to Bass Camp in June 1891.[48]

A noted travel writer, Charles Dudley Warner, took a trip from Flagstaff to the Grand Canyon in the summer of 1891, his account of the journey appearing in his book *Our Italy*, giving a fascinating glimpse of the nature of the trip. He noted, for instance, that,

> No work has been done on the road; it is made simply by driving over it. There are a few miles here and there of fair wheeling, but a good deal of it is intolerably dusty or exceedingly stony, and progress is slow.[49]

He described the trip as a, "tiresome journey of two days."[50] The trip was so hard, he said,

> A day of rest is absolutely required at the cañon, so that five days must be allowed for the trip. This will cost the traveller, according to the size of the party made up, from forty to fifty dollars.[51]

This was a considerable sum in those days, equal to about five hundred dollars today. As to the vehicle,

> Our party of seven was stowed in and on an old Concord coach drawn by six horses, and piled with camp equipage, bedding, and provisions. A four-horse team followed, loaded with other supplies and cooking utensils. The road lies on the east side of the San Francisco Mountain. Returning, we passed around its west side....[52]

On the way, the tourists camped in an unoccupied log cabin at East Cedar Ranch, "...a station of the Arizona Cattle Company."[53] They found water there. Continuing their journey in the morning, they next expected to find water at Red Horse, "...the only place where it is usually found in the day's march,"[54] but the well there was dry. At journey's end, they reached Hance's Camp, where,

> We descended into a hollow. There was the well, a log-cabin, a tent or two under the pine-trees. It was only to ascend the little steep, stony slope—thirty yards—and we should see [the Canyon]![55]

Warner's description of the trip shows that both the East and West Routes were in use, that all roads led to the water at East Cedar Ranch, that the next water stop was at Red Horse, and that the terminus was at Hance's Ranch. These were to be the essential ingredients of the forthcoming stage line, although the stage line would add a relay station at the Dillman Ranch in Hart Prairie on the Western Route.[56]

Another travel writer who took the trip in 1891 described it as follows,

> From Flagstaff it is some sixty-five miles, but it is a most enjoyable Summer trip through heavy pine country, over a fairly good road, and in a grass country. It means camping and some hardship, in any event, and should not be undertaken by invalids, or by ladies who are not accustomed to roughing it.[57]

Also in 1891, the railroad fever burst into flame again. There were public meetings in Flagstaff and it was announced that local men had raised $18,000, which they would offer, together with tax and other incentives, to any company that would construct a railroad line to the Grand Canyon. In order to provide a complete tourism package, the Flagstaff boosters proposed to build hotels at the Canyon, and even held talks with the Fred Harvey company about managing them.[58]

Later in the year 1891, the *Sun* told its readers that four Flagstaff prospectors, William Ashurst, [John] Marshall, [C. H.] McClure, and T. C. Frier, were building the Red Canyon Trail.[59]

The Grand Canyon-Flagstaff Stage Line

A Year-by-Year Account

1892

As 1892 dawned, there was more interest than ever before in the Grand Canyon. There had been so little snowfall during the winter that many parties of prospectors and tourists made their way to the South Rim even in the normally snowy season, January to March.[60]

One writer, who made the trip to the Grand Canyon at this time, was Horace Hovey, of the *Scientific American*. He appeared in Flagstaff in March but found that snow had finally fallen and that the roads were closed by heavy snow drifts. He came back in April and was able to make the journey then, hiring E. S. Wilcox to outfit him and act as guide. Hovey stated that while there were three points on the Atlantic & Pacific line from which one could initiate a trip to the Grand Canyon, Peach Springs, Williams, and Flagstaff, he thought the latter town was best suited for the purpose:[61]

> The Flagstaff route is somewhat longer than any of the others, being 67 miles by odometric measurement. This distance might be considerably shortened by a resurvey of the road, as it now makes some quite needless windings among the buttes and mesas. Its highest elevation above sea level is 7,436 feet and its lowest is 6,261 feet. These figures are official, having been taken under the direction of Mr. T. R. Gabel, superintendent of the Atlantic & Pacific at about the time of my own visit.[62]

Wilcox took Hovey over the Eastern Route, which Hovey reported to be the route chosen for the projected Flagstaff-Grand Canyon Railroad, "of which a beginning has already been made." He added, "Meanwhile, as I was told, a line of first-class coaches is to be immediately established." [As a side note to history buffs, Hovey stated that he saw the tree which gave Flagstaff its name still standing in the town. He gave no details about its location].

On the way out of town, Wilcox stopped and showed Hovey the Indian ruins at Old Caves Crater, giving the writer an intact pot he had found there. They stopped to eat at Jack Smith Tank, where they met T. R. Gabel of the Atlantic & Pacific and his surveying party returning to Flagstaff.

Hovey and Wilcox stopped for the night at East Cedar Ranch. At the ranch was a cabin where they found a few cowboys, "whose hospitality was ample, though primitive."

Crossing the valley, they went up Rabbit Canyon, the sides of which

Scientific American Magazine, Aug. 6, 1892

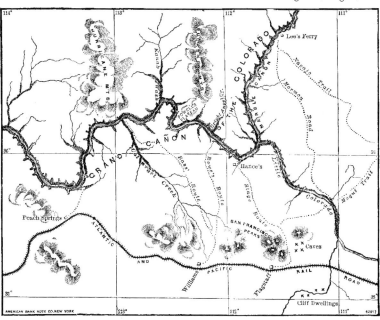

Map prepared by Horace Hovey at the time of his stage trip in April, 1892. It shows the Eastern Route, which he took. The Peach Springs and Williams stage lines are also depicted.

Hovey found remarkable, as the west side was composed of Aubrey[63] limestone and the east of lava. At the end of the day they reached Hance's cabin, "Under a sheltering hill, beside a living stream, nestled amid gigantic pines, some of which have been so felled as to fence in the spacious door yard...." He reported that the distance from the cabin to the rim was less than three hundred yards.

Hovey's experience was typical for travelers before the stage line began its operations. They had to hire a guide, horses, wagon and supplies, and spend a night in the open en route. The trip was slow, expensive, and uncomfortable. Such early travelers must have been heartened by what they were reading in the Flagstaff newspaper. The *Sun's* editor in January gleefully told his readers:

Titan of Chasms

Before the stage line: a private excursion

> As each week rolls by information of a more reliable nature as to the building of the Grand Canyon railroad is received. During the past week one of our citizens received a private letter from a prominent railroad official which concluded with the following significant sentence: "The Grand Canyon railroad will surely be built." We leave our readers to draw their own conclusions as to the meaning of these words.[64]

In March, the editor reported that the notion of a railroad was more than mere talk:

> Work was commenced on Saturday last on the Grand Canyon railroad at a point three miles east of here. Engineer Burns of the A. & P., is locating the grade and teams were put on Monday and are still at work. Just how much will be done at present is not known to the public, but it is hoped that work will be continued until the road is completed to the Grand Canyon, and trains running by the first of the year.[65]

[The Atlantic & Pacific Railroad, although it might have the superficial appearance of being an independent line, was a division of the Santa Fe,[66] so the newspaper called it the Atlantic & Pacific and the Santa Fe interchangeably].

In spite of these bold assurances, the Atlantic & Pacific did not built a railroad from Flagstaff to the Canyon. Officials of the railroad, however, were spending a great deal of time in and around Flagstaff, and it was clear that something big was in the air.[67] Though not yet announced publicly, the Atlantic & Pacific had decided to sponsor a stagecoach line from a town on the railroad to the Grand Canyon, and Flagstaff and Williams were both contenders for the honor.

In April 1892 Sanford Rowe, whom the *Sun* described as, "...the livery man of Williams, who takes tourists from Williams to the Grand Canyon," took T. R. Gabel, superintendent of the Atlantic & Pacific, from Williams to the Grand Canyon over the Williams wagon road, then looped around and took him to Flagstaff on the Flagstaff wagon road. T. A. Riordan, Flagstaff lumber mill co-owner and civic booster, went along on the ride.[68] Although the newspaper account of the trip did not say so, it would seem that Gabel was inspecting the virtues of the two routes, to determine which would be the better for the proposed stagecoach line. Perhaps Rowe and Riordan were acting as advocates, Rowe pointing out the features that favored Williams and Riordan espousing those in favor of Flagstaff, commenting on accommodations in the towns, the scenery on the way, the condition of the road, and so on.

Once they realized that there was a competition between the two towns, Flagstaff people hustled to convince Gabel that their city should be chosen.

The Flagstaff Board of Trade held a meeting on May 5 to discuss the question and a committee was appointed to study the cost of building accommodations for fifty people at the halfway point and at the Canyon.[69]

The *Sun* advised its readers of what was happening, as follows:

> For some time past the officials of the A. & P. railroad have been looking for a favorable route to the Grand Canyon from some point on their line which had enough local attractions to attract tourists, and from which the trip to the Grand Canyon could be easily made, and desiring that the citizens of some favorable point take action in the matter. Knowing the desire of the railroad management the Board of Trade, at its regular meeting, appointed a committee to interview T. R. Gabel...on the subject of making *Flagstaff the gateway to the Grand Canyon* [emphasis added]. Mr. Gabel stated that it was thought by the railway management that the citizens of any town desiring this important tourist traffic should be able to guarantee that all visitors would be taken care of in a first-class manner, and in consideration for this the railroad company would divert all of this class of travel to the point agreeing to furnish such accommodations.[70]

[The above reference is the first place in print where we saw the phrase, "Flagstaff, the gateway to the Grand Canyon" used].

The Board of Trade's committee took swift action, as described in the next edition of the *Sun*:

> Upon the report of the committee, the Board at once set to work to organize a stock company to build the necessary hotels at the half-way point and at the Canyon. Stock enough has been taken to secure the success of the undertaking and suitable accommodations for fifty visitors will be put up as soon as the material is on the ground.[71]

The Atlantic & Pacific seemed satisfied with the vigor and enterprise shown by the men of Flagstaff and chose Flagstaff to be the "gateway." Flagstaff officials said they would have the stage line and hotels ready in two weeks.[72]

True to their word, they immediately built a wood-frame midway house on the route,[73] at East Cedar Ranch, with its reliable water supply. This was the spot where Charles Dudley Warner had reported finding only an unoccupied log-house and stable for the Arizona Cattle Company's cowboys in 1891.[74] At the Canyon, accommodations were prepared at John Hance's ranch, which came to be called Hance's Camp. [It was at times referred to as the Canyon Hotel, and other names]. We could find no information about the arrangement that the stage line made with Hance, but it would have been customary business practice for Hance to charge rent or some other kind of fee for the use of his land, water, pasture, and trail.[75] In addition any revenues Hance might have received for these purposes, he guided tourists into the Canyon on his trail and rented animals, gear and his services.

The structure built by the railroad: the little white frame building to the left of the depot, front, left. It was the stage line's office

The structure built by the Flagstaff citizens' group: the "hotel" at East Cedar Ranch

Close-up of stage office west of depot

The Grand Canyon stage leaving Flagstaff. The open sides identify this as a type of coach called a mud wagon. Passengers ride on top, which was probably fun for the first hour, then palled considerably. What did they do when it rained? The passengers inside could roll down the canvas mud flaps

The appearance of the old road north of the Peaks

The management of the hotel division of the Grand Canyon-Flagstaff Stage Line was contracted to I. Chrisman, an experienced hotelier, who owned and operated the Del Monte Hotel in Flagstaff. Chrisman leased the halfway facility at East Cedar Ranch—where a relay exchange of horses would be made and passengers would eat lunch—to Frank E. Foster.[76]

With the lodging side of the business taken care of, arrangements for the transportation part of the stage line were made. A stage line office was constructed—probably by the railroad—just west of the depot, a free-standing little square building about 7 x 7 feet in floor width. E. S. Wilcox, who had operated the Grand Canyon livery stable business in Flagstaff for several years, was awarded the contract to run the stages. He provided the manpower, animal power and equipment, and the line began operation within two weeks of the meeting with Gabel, as promised.[77]

The *Sun* told its readers how the new Grand Canyon-Flagstaff Stage Line would operate in its May 12, 1892 issue:

> ...tourists, if they desire, can now make the trip to the canyon in a day. Stages for the present will leave Flagstaff on Monday, Wednesdays and Fridays. A hotel company, known as the Grand Canyon Hotel Company, has been incorporated for the purpose of building and carrying on the necessary eating houses on the route to the canyon. The officers of the company are Dr. D. J. Brannen, president; J. H. Hoskins, Jr, treasurer; H. D. Ross, secretary; George Babbitt, T. A. Riordan and P. J. Brannen directors. The management of the hotels has been let by contract to I. Chrisman, who will at once assume charge. The successful management of the stage line and the satisfactory management of the hotel is what the directors of the company will have to look after carefully, as on the direction of these depend largely the number of tourists who will visit the canyon from this point.[78]

The May 12 article stirred up a great deal of local interest and a clamor for more information. The *Sun* followed up in its next issue with another Grand Canyon Stage Line article:

> A good many letters of inquiry have been received by our citizens in regard to the Grand Canyon stage route from Flagstaff. The fare is $20 for the round trip. The stage leaves on Mondays, Wednesdays and Fridays, leaving Flagstaff at 7 o'clock a. m. and reaching the Canyon the same evening. Good hotel accommodations are to be had at the Canyon and at the halfway station at Cedar ranch. Parties of fifty visitors can be taken care of at the hotel at the Canyon. Now that the round trip can be made in three days without any preparation by visitors, there is a general enquiry for information, and a large number of people will visit the Grand Canyon of the Colorado this summer from this point.[79]

The first trip on the Grand Canyon-Flagstaff Stage Line was made on May 16, 1892. The Flagstaff Board of Trade invited W. A. Bissell, general passenger agent of the Atlantic & Pacific, to make the maiden run, with all his expenses paid, and told him that he could bring along two or three guests.[80]

Bissell accepted the offer and brought with him from Alameda, California, three friends: Dr. G. P. Reynolds, F. W. Van Sicklen, and T. G. Daniels, the editor of the *Alameda Daily Argus*. J. H. Hoskins Jr., a

Flagstaff banker and member of the Board of Trade, accompanied the group as its host.[81]

The trip went smoothly, with T. G. Daniels writing,

The ride from Flagstaff to the Grand Canyon, a matter of 65 to 70 miles, was altogether pleasant. We made it in one day. The road was level for the most part....

He also indicated that the accommodations at the Canyon were not really ready yet,

Two days spent in camp were the acme of enjoyment. We slept in the air and grew hearty and happy.[82]

Arriving at the Canyon on Monday, May 16, the initial group of travelers had Tuesday and Wednesday at leisure and spent their time wandering along the Rim from Hance's Camp. They seemed to feel that they were involved in a momentous occasion and that they should make their marks on history; so they named several points for themselves and their friends, including Bissell Point, Reynold's Lookout, and Gabel Point.[83]

NAU 90.10.1

Taken May 1892, by William Henry Jackson on one of the first runs of the new stage line, on the Eastern Route

When the group returned to Flagstaff on Thursday, May 19, Daniels' guests went back home, and were just in time to catch the westbound train. Daniels himself had business in the East, so he stayed in Flagstaff for a few hours and—working with the help of the editor of the *Sun*—sent the following dispatch to the Associated Press for distribution nationwide, a welcome bit of good publicity:

The new stage line from Flagstaff to the Grand Canyon was opened Monday by a trip made by W. A. Bissell and party, Dr. G. P. Reynolds, F. W. San Sicklen and T. G. Daniels, of Alameda, Cal., with J. H. Hoskins, Jr., representing the Flagstaff Board of Trade. The trip was made in eleven hours, fresh teams being provided at three relay stations. Everything passed off well, and the route is now open for regular business. Trips will be made three times a week, leaving Flagstaff Monday, Wednesday and Friday.[84]

In addition to the above dispatch, Daniels wrote several favorable articles that were published in West Coast newspapers and picked up by editors and reprinted around the country. The *Sun* printed a couple of these articles, one that Daniels wrote while he was in Flagstaff waiting for the train to go east, and another while he was on the train.[85]

Not content with this burst of genuine publicity, the editor of the *Sun* planted a bogus story in the paper headlined, "A Wild Girl Captured, Treed by Two Men, a Burro and a Dog, in the Grand Canyon." A tip-off to careful readers would have been the passage:

...Hance and I, had a pleasant unexpected experience that not often happens to the lot of man. Starting out early from the Grand Canyon Hotel, situated at the city of Hance, on the rugged edge of the Grand Canyon of the Colorado, at the end of the stage road leading from the city of Flagstaff, on the Atlantic & Pacific railroad, in Arizona, afoot, with a lunch prepared by the Cheerful Mrs. Murley, the mistress of the house, we entered the groves of cedars that skirt the wilds....[86]

Any Grand Canyon tale that included John Hance was automatically suspect, for Hance was a notorious spinner of tall tales. The story was a hit

Sherry G. Mangum

Holding the above Jackson photo in hand, we combed the area where we believed the Eastern Route ran for a match-up. Finally we found it. The old photo helped us locate the route. The vegetation looks different due to 100 years of fire suppression. Many of the spots that were bare in Jackson's day are now covered with young pine trees with readers, so the editor followed it up with a concluding article in a later issue. The Wild Girl, he claimed, when finally confronted and asked why she was roaming the Canyon in a perpetual state of lamentation replied, "Mam won't give me no 'lasses on my bread."[87]

Although the first stage line passengers reported that they slept in the open air, the hotel company immediately brought in tents for the tourists, and no other parties reported sleeping in the open.[88]

Railroad and stage line officials followed up the initial stage run with a number of other free trips designed to produce grist for their advertising mill. Charles Lummis, writer and promoter of the Southwest, and W. F. Clark of *St. Nicholas* magazine—a widely-read national journal—were given complimentary trips in the first week of the stage line's operation and went out on the second stage.[89] They signed Hance's guest book on May 21, 1892.[90] The Lummis party returned to Flagstaff just in time to meet the next bunch of promotional guests, a group consisting of Thomas Moran, the famous painter and his son, Paul; William Henry Jackson, noted photographer; and C. A. Higgins, Santa Fe advertising guru, who were bound for the Canyon, signing the guest book there on May 24, 1892.[91] The Santa Fe made an agreement with the painter Moran to pay all his expenses on the trip in return for the free use of one of his Grand Canyon paintings of their choice.[92] Jackson made a number of photographs that came to be regarded as standards, to be reproduced many times in the years following.[93] Higgins wrote several promotional books about the Grand Canyon for the Santa Fe.[94]

G. W. James

The Grand Canyon stage north of Flagstaff

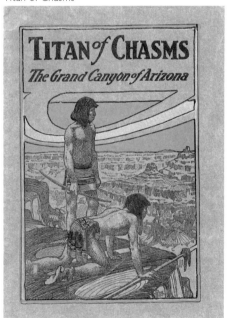

Titan of Chasms

Example of Railroad Advertising

Of his trip, Lummis wrote,

> And only now, for the first time in its history, is the Grand Cañon easily accessible to the traveler at its noblest point. A good stage line has just been started from Flagstaff, and I went out on the second trip, unwilling to advise travelers except from personal knowledge. Mr. Clark, of St. Nicholas, was with me. The road has been much improved since Mr. Warner's visit [in 1891], and is now the best long mountain-road in the southwest. There are comfortable hotels in Flagstaff, the stages are comfortable, the three relays of horses make the sixty-seven-mile journey easily in eleven hours, and there is nothing in the trip to deter ladies or young people. The drive is through the fine pine forests, with frequent and changing views of the noble San Francisco peaks and the Painted Desert. It brings one to the very brink of this terrific gorge almost without warning....[95]

It was clear from the outset that the line was going to be a success, and the Santa Fe supported the enterprise fully, turning out colorful brochures and other advertising materials. The railroad also ran heavily advertised special low excursion rates for the Fourth of July in 1892, a natural attraction in those days before air conditioning, when a trip to the cool Grand Canyon was a crowd-pleaser,[96] and over the years would sponsor any number of special fares and travel packages to stimulate travel to the Canyon.

By mid-July 1892 E. S. Wilcox was buying a bigger rig to meet the demands of the line, adding a stage with seven seats that was so big it was reported that it looked like a streetcar. His fleet was able to accommodate seventy-five passengers.[97] In September he bought yet another coach.[98]

Horace Hovey, who had traveled the route of the new stage line just before it opened, in April 1892, wrote again about the new and now-operational line, his article appearing in the August 6 issue of *Scientific American*,

> Since the first of May there has been a revolution worth chronicling. The Flagstaff board of trade, cooperating with the railroad officials, have decided at last to make the Grand Canyon accessible to tourists. Tri-weekly coaches, with relays of horses, are now run by Wilcox in a single day to the head of the Hance trail, where

a first-class hotel is being erected with accommodations for fifty guests. This news is told pro bono publico, and will be appreciated by those who have had to make the trip by buckboard or wagon, with primitive log cabin accommodations.[99]

When Hovey wrote that a first-class hotel was being erected, he was relying on representations made to him by the personnel of the stage line. The proposed and ballyhooed hotel was never built, and accommodations at the Canyon at Hance Camp never rose above the level of tents. This lack of a first-class hotel was to become a sore point of increasing significance over the years.

Almost coincident with the inauguration of the stage line, was another nibble at a railroad from Flagstaff to the Grand Canyon. In mid-June a number of well-heeled capitalists from the Midwest and East Coast appeared in Flagstaff to look over the situation and evaluate the proposition. The group included people familiar to Flagstaff stockmen, as they were principals in the Arizona Cattle Company.[100] Again, however, it was a false alarm, and the group decided not to make the investment.

In the busy summer of 1892, Pete Berry, Ralph and Niles Cameron, Bob Ferguson, and Ed Gale began the construction of the Grandview Trail down to their Last Chance Mine in July. On top of the Rim they located a 5-acre mill site about two miles (in a direct line) west of Hance's Camp, and before long had built a log cabin on it.[101] This operation, in time, would have a bearing on the stage line.

Grand Canyon of the Colorado

Moran's sketch of tourists on the Hance Trail

By August, the *Sun* was happy to advise its readers,

The Grand Canon of the Colorado river is receiving considerable attention through the eastern press, and Flagstaff is the point from which all visitors are directed to reach the now much talked of wonder of the world.[102]

The fame of the Grand Canyon as a tourist attraction was spreading beyond the United States, and foreign visitors became increasingly common. One foreign visitor who caught the attention of the editor of the Sun was an unnamed English minister "from some place near London," who appeared in Flagstaff in July, stating that he was going to walk to the Grand Canyon. The reason given by the tourist for the tramp was that he did not have funds enough to pay the stage fare, and he must see the Grand Canyon.[103] The implication of the article was that if the Grand Canyon were worth walking to, it was surely worth a stagecoach ride.

GCM 5305

The Buffalo Bill party hamming it up. John Hance on the far right. Bill is to his left. Taken near Hance Camp.

The flames of interest in the Grand Canyon were fanned even higher near the end of 1892 when Buffalo Bill, leading a large party of guests that was originally assembled in London, made a highly publicized trip to the Grand Canyon in November. The party while in Flagstaff stayed at the Del Monte Hotel, owned and operated by Isaac Chrisman, who was the manager of lodgings for the stage line. The *Sun* reported,

Thursday night the company spent the time going about town taking in the sights. They were highly pleased with the attention and civility everywhere shown them and voted Flagstaff the best town they had yet struck.[104]

The group included Major John M. Burke, who had been with Custer at the Little Big Horn and was one of a handful of survivors of the battle; Col.

The first relay station 1892-1895. This structure on the former Dillman Ranch is the only surviving building of any kind on the stage route. Taken in September 1998

Prentiss Ingraham, prolific author of dime novels glorifying Cody and other Western heroes; and R. C. Haslam, a legendary pony express rider who wore out thirteen horses on an epic ride of 120 miles, carrying the news of Lincoln's election, so that a gambler could win a $200,000 election bet. The party also included a veteran of the Civil War—wounded at Antietam—and Englishmen who had been through the Crimean War and the Sepoy Mutiny.[105]

After their stay in Flagstaff, where they hired horses and wagons, Cody's party went to the South Rim, signing the guest book at Hance's Camp on November 14. John Hance showed them around the South Rim, proudly posing for a photograph with the party out on the tip of a dangerous ledge, and began collecting Buffalo Bill memorabilia. Following a short stay at the South Rim, some of the party returned to Flagstaff, while Cody and others went up into Utah and over to the North Rim.[106, 107]

Winter weather brought the inaugural year of the stage line to a close in November 1892.[108] John Hance's guest book was signed by three hundred and two tourists after May 16.[109] In the similar period for 1891, only one hundred and sixty-three guests signed the book, so the stage line and the publicity surrounding it had almost doubled business.[110]

1893

Antelope Valley as seen by Sharlot Hall. Today the area is covered by subdivisions

In 1893, the Grand Canyon-Flagstaff Stage Line had a typical opening date, with its season beginning the first of April, On April 2, 1893, tourists from Chicago and New York signed Hance's guest book noting, "We are reported the first visitors of the season...."[111]

The line conducted business with the same personnel that it had in 1892 until July, when Lyman H. Tolfree came from Bakersfield to replace Isaac Chrisman as manager of the hotel side of the stage line operation.[112] Tolfree was described as, "...the well-known proprietor of the railroad hotels at Mojave, Bakersfield and Saugus...."[113]

The stage line made its initial appearance in a valued guidebook, *Baedeker's United States.* This German publication enjoyed such a sterling reputation in Europe that the company decided to prepare an English-language guide to America both for European and native visitors. Its description of the Grand Canyon-Flagstaff Stage Line, though terse, was typically accurate:

The Western Route, just north of today's Museum of Northern Arizona

> Flagstaff (6935 ft.; Hotels) is of importance as the starting-point of the main stage-route to (65 M.) the Grand Cañon of the Colorado (see below)....

> The stage-coaches from Flagstaff to the (65 M.) Grand Cañon (fair road) run tri-weekly (except in winter) in 12 hrs. (return-fare $20). Dinner ($1) is provided at a half-way house, and the road ends, near the cañon, at Hance's Camp, with comfortable, wooden-floored tents (meals $1; lodging $1; hotel to be built).[114]

Sharlot Hall, who was later to become the Arizona territorial and state historian, made a private trip from Prescott to the Grand Canyon in July 1893. Her diary contains some interesting comments about what she saw concerning the stage line. She took the Western Route and described the appearance of the first part of the journey as it would have been seen by a stagecoach passenger.

> Leaving the town we followed the stage road out through Potato Valley [later called Antelope Valley], a rather pretty, long, narrow,

valley bordered by high mountains and pine forests. Here the trees have been butchered in a shameful manner. Acres and acres of great pines are sawed up into lengths ready for loading and left to rot on the ground. All the mills have been moved away and the timber that would make millions of feet of lumber is left to rot.[115]

She and her party camped at Little Spring, where they saw a group of German army officers returning from the Canyon. The coach must have stopped at the camping spot, because Sharlot posted some mail with the driver.

After Little Spring, Ms. Hall resumed the journey, describing the next leg:

Left camp early this morning and took the road for the Grand Cañon. Travelled for the first few miles through a forest of grand pine trees skirting the northern base of San Francisco peak. The road passed through a bit of level land bordered on each side by low hills of volcanic origins.....There must be more than a hundred of these craters along our road. Gradually we leave the pine and come into a forest of cedars and fifteen miles from Little Springs, we leave most of the timber behind. From this point we have a view of a long stretch of barren country, round volcanic mountains and narrow open valleys extending to the Little Colorado River. Here the ground is as bare as a floor, hardly the grass roots are left.[116]

Hall was describing the view northward from the flank of Missouri Bill Hill. She continued,

Passing Klostermyres [sic Klostermeyer's] we go on three and a half miles to Hull's ranch [East Cedar Ranch]. This is a station on the stage line and a ranch of the A-1 Cattle Company. The water which we found in many long log troughs is piped down from a spring up on the mountains. Here we found that the old road to the Cañon was abandoned and, starting from Hull's ranch, there is a stretch of twenty-two miles without water. We watered the stock, had dinner, filled all our water kegs and moved on.[117]

From East Cedar Ranch she recorded her impressions of the next part of the journey:

We made a drive of ten or fifteen miles and went into camp—a dry camp—just at the edge of a cedar forest. We can see beyond us the far-away blue line of Coconino Forest. No large mountains are in sight as we have dropped below San Francisco and crossed a hill which hides it from view. We are encamped in a little basin where the horses have very good grass but no water except what we have hauled. All around us are small cedars.

We were gradually going up grade all that time and at last the cedars gave place to piñon pine and, after passing Moqui station, to pine. [Moqui] station is midway between Hull's ranch and the Cañon. The water supply consists of a large tank which is filled by the rains. After leaving the station we travelled all afternoon through heavy pine timber—the Coconino Forest. After hours of travel through this seemingly endless forest we came up on a high hill and caught a glimpse of the Grand Cañon. These views were grand indeed but we hurried on to make camp at a point where a trail goes down [the Grandview].[118]

It is interesting that she mentions Moqui station. Before 1892, the stop that travelers made after leaving Cedar Ranch was at Red Horse. Warner had reported finding Red Horse dry when he took his trip in 1891. We believe that the stage line operators created Moqui station in 1892 in order to have a reliable water source where it was most needed. Moqui is almost exactly halfway between East Cedar and Hance's Camp, whereas Red

Ft. Valley north of Flagstaff, as seen by the travelers

Fort Moroni, the old Mormon fort that gave Fort Valley its name. It was seen by passengers on the way out of Flagstaff. The valley was uninhabited in 1902, but is today full of homes

Approaching Hart Prairie

Hart Prairie, one of the loveliest spots on the trip

Buckboard north of East Cedar Ranch

The troughs at Little Spring. For the 1896 season, the stage line moved its first relay station to Little Spring and constructed some buildings there. These were torn down in the 1960s.

Horse was several miles farther toward the Canyon.

Sharlot Hall's descriptions are quite accurate, easily followed today, and give a good idea of the traveler's experience except for two things: first, the stage coach would have made its first relay stop after leaving Flagstaff at the Dillman Ranch in the shadow of Fern Mountain, in the Hart Prairie area; second, it would have ended the journey at Hance's Camp rather than at Grandview.

Another traveler who went to the Canyon in 1893 and described the trip was Flagstaff pioneer George Hochderffer, who recalled the event in his autobiography *Flagstaff Whoa.* He and his brother Will and their wives hired a coach from J. W. Thurber, who kept a livery stable in Flagstaff. Hochderffer described the first portion of the trip thus,

> Driving from Flagstaff over the old road, stopping to water the horses at Leroux Springs trough, then passing over the bluff through Hart Prairie and along the foot of Humphrey Peak and down through the quaking aspens just past Little Spring....[119]

The authors are convinced that Hochderffer's reference to the "old road" meant the Beale Road, built in 1858 and 1859, which he would have taken to a point at the north end of Fort Valley, departing from it there.

They camped overnight, then made another few miles the next day:

> Early next morning we set out upon our way. At that time the old stage road, known as the Tuba City road, passed upon the east side of Walker Lake, through what was then known as Horse Thief Pass. A small log cabin by the roadside at the entrance to the pass was said to have been occupied at one time by Mormon horse thieves. This hut was also known as Horse Thief Cabin. That second night we went into camp early at Lockett's Tanks, later called Moqui. Here also was a cabin called Horse Thief Cabin.[120]

The third day out, the Hochderffers reached their destination,

> The next day we drove to the canyon.....Those who have never traveled over the old stage road to the Grand Canyon and have never seen John Hance at his old lookout will never know what they have missed.[121]

Another Flagstaff to Grand Canyon traveler in 1893, Henry Finck, took the stage and wrote two articles about his trip for *Nation* magazine. Some of his observations help fill out the details about the journey and the operation of the stage line.

> The trip from Flagstaff is somewhat fatiguing on account of its length, and the heat and dust; yet the dust is not as persistent and annoying as on the way to the Yosemite, and the heat is often mitigated by a brisk breeze, in which warm blasts from the Painted Desert of the Little Colorado alternate oddly with cool waves from the San Francisco Mountain. The road bed is usually level and smooth, except here and there where we traverse one of those stony patches that abound in volcanic regions, and where the ground is roughened with igneous rocks.[122]

Finck casts valuable light on the way the stage line used the two routes, East and West:

> Those who take their own team and camping-outfit can make the complete circuit of the mountain by keeping to its left on the way home [Eastern Route]; but the stage has to retrace its course [Western route], on account of the relays of horses, which cannot be kept on both sides.[123]

Although the press releases for the stage line talked about hotels midway and at the Canyon, Finck found things much more primitive:

> Along the stage-road from Flagstaff to the Cañon... [were] the sta-

tions where we changed horses, and which consisted merely of a stable for the horses, a tent for the man in charge, and a lonely dog....[124]

At the end of the line, Finck found,

Ten hours and a half after leaving Flagstaff, we reach the Grand Cañon Station [Hance's Camp], which at present consists of a log-cabin (stored with bacon, hams, canned goods, and antidotes to thirst), besides a number of tents—a large one for kitchen and dining-room, and smaller ones for visitors, each tent having a board floor and a comfortable bed. The tents cost a dollar a day, and the same sum is charged for a meal, which will be found as good as can be expected under the circumstances. Through a lucky coincidence, two of the very few springs on the Cañon's brink were found right here, where the scenery is at its best.[125]

Most visitors to the Grand Canyon were enchanted by John Hance, and Finck was no exception. He noted:

No visitor to this region should fail to place himself for a day or two under the guidance of Mr. John Hance, who has for nine years made the Cañon his home, and knows every accessible part of it as well as you know your own house. He has asbestos, copper, and silver mines—fifty-eight in number—in various parts of it, has one cabin on the brink, another part way down, and another by the river, with plenty of burros for himself and those who intrust themselves to his care....[126]

We believe that the "cabin on the brink" referred to Hance's new cabin at the head of the Old Hance Trail.

Hance acted as a guide along the Rim for Finck:

If you lack time or strength to follow Mr. Hance into this strange abyss, you must not fail, at any rate, to go with him to Bissell's Point, five miles east of the camp, or, better still, a mile less, to a sort of isolated buttress or rocky projection, whence you see straight down the abrupt wall....[127]

An economic depression known as the Panic of '93 hit Wall Street during the second season for the stage line, and the results slowly filtered out into the hinterlands. In part the crash was caused by the free-trade position taken by President Cleveland, who had been elected in 1892. One of the planks of his reform platform was the abolition of the tariff on wool, which was bad news to Flagstaff, the number one industry of which was sheep ranching. By August 1893 the depression had such an impact on the economy that the Atlantic & Pacific Railroad could not pay wages due its workers and had to defer payday for three weeks.[128] The *Sun* would report at the end of the year, that, "The year 1893 will be remembered by the citizens of Flagstaff as the dullest in the annals of its history."[129]

A distinguished passenger took the Grand Canyon-Flagstaff Stage Line in August 1893, none other than Major John Wesley Powell, the man who brought the Grand Canyon to the attention of the world when he made his heroic Colorado river expedition in 1869. Powell was accompanied by his wife and daughter, and while the trio were in Flagstaff, they were the guests of lumber baron D. M. Riordan.[130]

Isaac Chrisman, the Flagstaff hotel-keeper who originally had charge of

MNA MS 196-74-1986

Moqui Relay Station

MNA MS 196-74-1989

Red Horse. Ralph Cameron is reported to have moved a building from Red Horse to the Village circa 1900. It became the foundation for his hotel building

GCM 669

The Cameron Hotel, later the Post Office. Ralph Cameron used the building he removed from Red Horse as the lower story. Could it have been the structure in the photo above?

Land of Sunshine

The Bank Hotel in Flagstaff. This photograph is well-known and has caused more than one historian to reach erroneous conclusions. The vehicle is not a stagecoach. The long wheelbase would have made it totally unsuitable for the stage line's roads. It was a depot wagon, which was used to take passengers and luggage from the train station to the hotels. Other writers who saw this photo concluded that the hotel was the terminus of the stage line. Advertising copy used by the hotel boasted that the stage started at the hotel, which was true in a way; but the hotel was not the terminus. The terminus, in fact, was at the depot

Homes Travelogues

A Concord coach. This elegant, durable vehicle was the queen on rough Western roads, carrying passengers, freight and mail with reliability and relative comfort. These coaches usually had waist-high doors with windows. This model has been specially modified for sightseeing purposes

the hotels for the stage line before relinquishing the post to L. H. Tolfree in July 1893, suffered a huge loss in September 1893 when his Del Monte Hotel, also called the Tourist Hotel, situated on the northwest corner of Birch Avenue and San Francisco Street in Flagstaff, burned to the ground. Before the fire, it seemed that Chrisman was poised to take advantage of the hotel traffic generated by the line, as shown by the fact that Buffalo Bill and his party stayed at the Del Monte in 1892; but the fire ruined Chrisman, and he did not rebuild.[131] After the fire, there was only one hotel for Grand Canyon tourists in Flagstaff, the Bank Hotel at the corner of Leroux Street and Railroad Avenue. The Hawks Hotel just north of the railroad depot was also in business, but it was really a boarding house and did not cater to overnight guests. Some modern writers have claimed that the Bank Hotel was the terminus of the stage line, but we believe that the news accounts, descriptions by travelers, and other evidence make it clear that the terminus was at the stage line office a few feet west of the depot.

Flagstaff residents, always keen to have a railroad from their town to the Grand Canyon, had been watching with interest the fate of a short line railroad to the west, the Prescott and Arizona Central Railway. Running from Seligman to Prescott, it had been built on a shoestring in 1886 and was plagued by perpetual bad service and the arrogant indifference of its owner. Its poor service had created a competitive opportunity, which was taken up in 1892 when a rival railroad, the Santa Fe, Prescott & Phoenix, built a line from Ash Fork to Prescott, nicknamed The Peavine, which began operations in April 1893. By October 1893, the Peavine had put the Prescott and Arizona Central out of business.[132] C. M. Funston, the editor of the *Sun*, immediately opined that this defunct railroad might create an opportunity to build a railroad from Flagstaff to the Grand Canyon, as the rails and rolling stock of the P. A. C. could be picked up at bargain prices.[133] Nothing came of the idea.

In spite of the Wall Street Panic, the 1893 season turned out to be a good one for the stage line. Travel was up over the year before, with sixty-seven passengers making the run in the month of September alone.[134] The line closed for the winter on November 1.[135]

William Hull, who still had a hand in Grand Canyon tourism, teamed together with L. H. Tolfree in November 1893 to lease the Old Hance Trail from John Hance for a five year period for a payment of three hundred dollars per year.[136] The details of this arrangement were not reported. Tolfree, of course, was the manager of the hotel service for the Grand Canyon-Flagstaff Stage Line, while Hull had no connection with the line. Perhaps Tolfree and Hull were trying to develop the Hull Ranch, located about a mile south of Hance Camp, as a tourist camp for people who came to the Canyon by their own means. Even so, this might have put him in competition with the facilities at Hance Camp, a serious conflict of interest. It is clear that stage line passengers staying at Hance Camp continued to use the Old Hance Trail, with Hance as their guide, so the import of this lease remains hazy.

In December 1893 the Coconino County Board of Supervisors decided to do their bit to promote tourism. They appropriated money to repair the Eastern Route, authorizing Robert A. Ferguson to do the work. One doesn't know whether to cheer or laugh at their action, for the amount they coughed up was fifty dollars, a paltry sum for road repair even in those days.[137]

1894

In March of 1894, T. R. Gabel, the superintendent of the Atlantic & Pacific Railroad, announced in the *Sun* that the stagecoach line would open for the year as soon as spring weather would permit.[138] E. S. Wilcox notified townspeople that he was displaying at the stagecoach office a print of a painting that Thomas Moran had made of the Canyon depicting Hance's trailhead, a painting produced when Moran was given a free trip during the stage line's first week of operation in 1892. The railroad had turned the painting into a widely-circulated lithograph for advertising purposes,[139] having it carefully reproduced by the finest printing process and sumptuously mounted in gilt frames. The stages began running on May 1, in 1894, with L. H. Tolfree in charge of the lodgings at East Cedar Ranch and at the Canyon.[140]

A freelance operator, J. W. Thurber, made a bid to take advantage of the Grand Canyon travel boom. He bought the stables and corrals of William Dickerson on East Aspen Avenue and gave notice that he was going to develop it into a first-class operation.[141] Soon he was notifying travelers that he had the best teams and rigs in the country and would take tourists to the Grand Canyon with guides.[142] Another independent stage service was created by I. F. Wheeler, of whom we shall see more later. He told prospective travelers that he could make the trip from Flagstaff to the Canyon in one day, with a single change of horses at East Cedar Ranch.[143]

The main stage line, however, had the lion's share of the tourist business, and it enjoyed a good start to its 1894 season, boosting the appearance

MNA MS 196-74-2000

On the Hance Trail

America Remembered

Concord coach, with its thoroughbrace suspension. This is the coach most often seen in Western movies. Note the waist-high doors. These coaches were built with strong roofs so that passengers could sit topside

Stoddard's Lectures

Another view of a crowded Concord

Munk, Arizona Sketches

John Hance in front of the new cabin built for him by the stage line. It was made of milled lumber and was located at the head of the Old Hance Trail

of its quarters by adding a curio room full of Indian art and artifacts in the office building.[144]

The *Sun* used the phrase, "Flagstaff is the gateway to the Grand Canyon..." again in its May 17, 1894 issue.[145] It was a catchy slogan, and probably of value for advertising purposes.

In May E. S. Wilcox, the operator of the stage line, appeared before the Coconino County Board of Supervisors and requested that the county improve the road to the Grand Canyon. The Board deferred action, directing its clerk to confer with T. R. Gabel, superintendent of the Atlantic & Pacific Railroad.[146]

The Atlantic & Pacific was in no shape to spend money for the improvement of the stagecoach road. Although the stage line itself was doing well in the summer of 1894, the railroad, which had been somewhat shaky from its beginning because of the long empty hauls it had to make through sparsely settled Arizona and New Mexico, was not strong enough to withstand the loss of business caused by the Panic of '93 and went into receivership in July 1894.[147] The receivers kept the railroad running, however, with little discernible change in the support it gave to the Grand Canyon-Flagstaff Stage Line.

In 1894 the bicycle craze, which had earlier swept the more settled sections of the country, reached Flagstaff. It was inevitable that bike riders should set their sights on the trip from Flagstaff to the Grand Canyon. After all, a fit cyclist could go as fast as a team of horses, and by using the stagecoach route, would have good roads to follow. The first reported trip by bicycle from Flagstaff to the Grand Canyon was on August 24, 1894, when a group of six local riders initiated the run.[148] A separate chapter is devoted to bicycling from Flagstaff to the Grand Canyon, so only a brief mention of it is given here.

E. S. Wilcox put on a new thoroughbrace[149] coach with seats for nine passengers for the 1894 season.[150] Presumably, this was one of the big Concord coaches, which offered a superior ride. Wilcox also remodeled the stage line's office, and filled it with Indian curios and souvenirs.[151] A post office named Tolfree—with L. H. Tolfree as postmaster—was created at Hance's Camp for the convenience of travelers, an indication that travel was still brisk and that the stage line carried mail as well as passengers.[152]

By September it was reported that travel to the Grand Canyon had been very heavy.[153]

In November 1894, the *Sun* carried an exciting story,

A press report from New York says the Santa Fe Railroad has decided to make Flagstaff the leading mountain resort on its lines. A railway will be built from Flagstaff to the Grand Canyon of the Colorado, the greatest natural wonder of the world, and through railroad tickets to Grand Canyon station will be on sale from all principal points at special rates, with stopover privileges at Flagstaff. From there the company will transport tourists in an old-fashioned Concord four-horse coach to the famous cliff and cave dwellings. Oak Creek trout fishing grounds and other points of interest. A $300,000 hotel is to be erected at Flagstaff to accommodate the tourists.

In spite of the optimistic announcement, nothing happened to turn this idea into a reality.[154] There was more railroad talk, this time of a line to the Grand Canyon from Williams, and it was reported that J. A. Lamport [see below] was making a preliminary survey for the proposed line, the cost of the survey being paid by citizens of Williams.[155] This too came to naught.

The Grand Canyon-Flagstaff Stage Line was able to run almost to Thanksgiving in 1894 before Wilcox shut it down due to bad weather.[156] In its third year of operation, in spite of a national recession and the difficulties of its affiliated railroad, it was still running profitably.

December saw an upsetting announcement, when the *Sun* carried the story that T. R. Gabel, who for several years had been the superintendent of the Atlantic & Pacific Railroad, was going to resign. Gabel was the man who had overseen the creation of the Grand Canyon-Flagstaff Stage Line and was its staunch supporter. Gabel's successor was to be Arthur Wells, and Flagstaff boosters lost no time cultivating his friendship. D. M. Riordan took him to the Grand Canyon as soon as the news was announced, then accompanied him to Albuquerque and showed him the other sights of Flagstaff.[157]

The Coconino County Surveyor, J. A. Lamport, who had previously been a partner with J. R. Treat in an early Flagstaff-Grand Canyon stage line, prepared a map showing the Western Route for its first twenty-two miles. This map was duly filed in the county records, where it can still be found.[158]

1895

James Wilbur Thurber and family. Although E. S. Wilcox (no photo available) got the stagecoach started, it was Thurber who made most of its innovations and brought it to prominence

In 1895, J. W. Thurber became the most significant individual in the operation of the Grand Canyon-Flagstaff Stage Line when the Atlantic & Pacific entered into a contract with him to run the coaches, replacing E. W. Wilcox.[159] Although Thurber wanted a longer term, the Atlantic & Pacific could only offer him a single-year contract due to its receivership proceedings, still underway. The railroad also pushed Thurber to buy John Hance's trail rights and obtain from Hance a covenant not to compete in the Grand Canyon tourist business.[160]

As soon as Thurber took over management he immediately acquired new equipment to assure tourists of better travel conditions, including an "easy riding stage."[161] Thurber kept his animals and vehicles at his livery stable at the east end of Aspen Avenue and continued to use the little building west of the depot as the stage line's office. He made no changes in the personnel operating the hotel side of the stage line, which remained in the hands of L. H. Tolfree, who lived at the Canyon during the tourist season with his wife and two daughters, Edith and Gertrude.

Thurber began running coaches to the Canyon on April 6 in 1895.[162] The *Sun* carried a detailed account of one of Thurber's first trips—on the Eastern Route—written by a California newspaper editor:

> The Grand Canyon stage, with the masterful hand of Ike Wheeler at the reins, rumbled out of town on its first trip of the season last Monday morning, carrying three passengers, who looked for the first time on the grandest sight in all the world. The ride at this season is thoroughly invigorating, and the roads are in excellent condition, being for the most part hard and comparatively free from dust.
>
> As the carryall rolls along through the almost interminable forests of graceful pines and gently perfumed cedars, waving their incense to the winds, and on under the shadow of the snow-tipped peaks, glowing in their dress of white and flashing their radiance toward the sky, the mind is freshened and prepared in a measure for the contemplation of Nature's sublime masterpiece. Now you are bowling along the side of a pine-clad hill, now plunging down toward the gray billows of sand that [are] in markedly striking relief to the fierce beauty of the Sunset Crater, with its lava-strewn sides and crimson cap, still threatening its little world with its red glare and menacing frown.
>
> With fresh relays of horses at three different stations you dash on until finally the little white canvas village appears in the gloom of twilight. There you are made heartily welcome by Landlord L. H. Tolfree and his estimable wife and interesting daughters and assigned to a snowy tent in the sylvan shades. The excellent host

In the foreground, right, is the livery stable and corral owned by J. W. Thurber. Located at the northeast corner of Aspen Avenue and Agassiz Street, it was only a block from the stage line's terminus at the depot, so it was an easy matter for Thurber to move his animals and vehicles back and forth from the terminus to the stables.

had only been on the ground a few days, yet everything was in shipshape, and the accommodations would bear comparison with those offered in a palatial city hotel. A first-class chef presides over the kitchen, and visitors this year may expect the menu to be not the least of the pleasant memories of their trip....

This great wonder promises to attract more sightseers this year than ever before in its history. J. W. Thurber, manager of the stage line, has already made arrangements for the transportation of several parties of tourists and townspeople. Under his management the line cannot fail to become popular. He is enterprising, accommodating and always alive to the comfort of his patrons, and deserves well.[163]

An English tourist who took the trip gave his impressions in a newspaper article:

We alighted from a splendid Pullman coach at Flagstaff station, a remarkably pretty little town in northern Arizona and the only place of any note we encountered after leaving Albuquerque, N. M.

Securing hotel accommodations, which we found to be of as good a class as anything we encountered in many of the large cities in the east and at reasonable rates, the next morning, we boarded a stage making tri-weekly trips to the Grand Canyon of the Colorado.

The trip to the Canyon took eleven hours. The stage road passes through some of the prettiest and most picturesque scenery I have seen....

The stage reached the camp near the canyon at 6 o'clock p. m. and we all tumbled out, overjoyed that the journey was ended....

Captain John Hance [invited] us to his cabin and we are entertained by this delightful character until far into the evening. He would keep us up all night telling us his wonderful experience....[164]

Col. H. G. Otis of the *Los Angeles Times* took the stage on May 29, 1895, with a party of bigwigs from the Santa Fe, the ensemble traveling to Flagstaff in the private railroad car of one of the officials. They traveled via the Western Route, and Otis wrote:

The two four-in-hand stages of Thurber's line got off for the canyon at 7 o'clock in the morning in gallant style. The tough and wiry Arizona horses know the road, and in the hands of skillful and safe drivers the coaches make good time—an average of six miles an hour over the whole distance of seventy miles.

The first portion of the journey is through a somewhat open country, where are to be seen a few cultivated fields, fenced with strong, well-built log or "worm" fences, with an occasional frame casa and numerous comfortable log houses, some of them of hewed logs, but most of them au naturel....

On the lower slopes of the mountain, along its westerly flanks, where the stage road runs, the soil shows an excellent quality, and some progress has been made in farming....

The road from Flagstaff to the Grand Canyon runs largely through a much more flat and even country than is popularly supposed. There are no difficult ascents or descents, and for a natural road it is an exceptionally good one. In very few places has any work been required upon it....

The camp lies in a little depression near the rim of the canyon,

Stoddard's Lectures

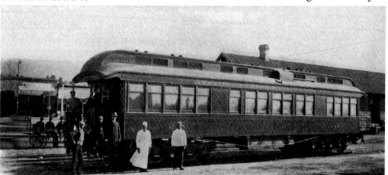

A Pullman car at the Flagstaff depot. The stage line office is out of sight behind the car. For passengers coming in from the East, a Pullman would arrive in town at night, be shunted off to a side track, as seen here, and serve as a hotel for the guests, who had to walk only a few feet to the office the next morning to begin their journey to the Canyon

which cannot be seen at all from the camp. Two minutes' walk, however, carries the beholder up another short slope, and suddenly the awful majesty of the Grand Canyon is revealed to his startled vision....

The air was raw and cold, but the fire in Hance's log cabin roared cheerily; the provender in the Tolfree dining-room was ample and toothsome; we had appetites...which were worth going miles to secure; Mr. Tolfree, wife and bright daughters were hospitable and attentive; the cots in the tent bedrooms were covered with a great abundance of Navajo and other blankets....[165]

I was fortunate in having for chaperone and guide [for exploration the next day] one of the bright young daughters of our host of the hostelry.... Miss Edith[166] wore a riding costume that was most appropriate....

From Hance's Point, where the truth-telling "big-horn" hunter-guide has built his newest cabin, perched upon the edge of the abyss, we enjoyed our first wide-extended view of the canyon....

Los Angeles Times

Edith Tolfree by Times artist Chapin

The author concluded his article by suggesting that improvements should be built at the Camp: it needed, he said, a real hotel, and suggested a big rustic log lodge, furnished simply, with animal skins and Navajo rugs on its floors.[167] Such a lodge is exactly what Pete Berry would build in 1896, but at Grandview, not at Thurber's Camp.

The summer of 1895 was a busy one for travel writers. The Editorial Association of Southern California worked out a special travel package for its members whereby they could travel round-trip to Flagstaff from Los Angeles, then take the stage to the Canyon, all for twenty dollars per person. C. M. Funston, the editor of the *Coconino Weekly Sun*, was all a-twitter at the prospect of showing off the virtues of Flagstaff and his newspaper to his peers and gave extensive coverage of the event, before, during, and after, in the pages of the *Sun*.[168] The travel package was so attractive that Funston predicted some seventy-five persons would take advantage of it.[169] The day before the group arrived, he lowered his projection to forty people.[170] When the group appeared on June 7, it was learned that only twenty-three had made the trip, and that not all were journalists, some being spouses and guests. Still, the sojourners represented about a dozen West Coast periodicals, and the members of the Flagstaff Board of Trade rolled out the red carpet for them. On their first day, spent in Flagstaff, they were treated to a trip to the Arizona Lumber and Timber Company, where they watched logs being sawed; this was followed by a trip to the rock quarry; then Walnut Canyon; then the day was wrapped up with a grand ball at the Bank Hotel, where they were staying. The next day they rode the Grand Canyon-Flagstaff Stage Line to Hance's Camp, where they stayed three days, and were enchanted both by the Canyon and John Hance.[171] The pen-pushers had a first-rate time and responded positively to the experience, giving improvised college-type yells from their train car as they left town, " Flagstaff! Flagstaff! Rah! Rah! Rah!"[172] Editor Funston summarized,

Los Angeles Times

Gertrude Tolfree, sketch by the same artist

The visit to Flagstaff of the leading members of the Editorial Association of Southern California cannot fail to benefit the town. If newspaper advertising pays—and we hold that there is no better method of advertising in the world—then the value of the editors' visit and their hearty reception and entertainment will be almost incalculable, because each one of the party will write of his trip, and Flagstaff 's fame as an ideal summer resort, and the gorgeous scenery almost at her gates, will be extolled at length in the various publications represented. There were some talented magazine writers among the visitors and we can expect that Flagstaff will be muchly written of this summer.[173]

An old hand at travel to the Grand Canyon, Charles Lummis, made the trip again in 1895 and produced an article in which he said,

G. W. James

The twenty-four troughs at East Cedar Ranch

It is so easily reached that there is no pardon for them who neglect it. The Pullmans of the Santa Fe overland carry one to Flagstaff, Arizona, the growing town among the pines at the foot of Mt. Agassiz; and thence a comfortable stage-ride brings one to the camp on the very verge of the Cañon. There is no hardship about it. Adequate accommodations are there....[174]

Writer G. A. Neeff took the trip in the summer of 1895. He counted the eye-catching log-troughs at East Cedar Ranch and found that there were twenty-four of them. About his adventure he wrote,

We use the road to the left, the west side of San Francisco Peak. After a ride of 18 miles the first relay station at Little Springs is reached, and then a 16-mile trot brings us to the dinner station at Cedar Ranch. Here Mrs. Klostermeyer serves an elegant meal and then the most tedious part of the journey, 23 miles, is encountered; when at five o'clock the last four-in-hand takes us from Moqui station through the beautiful Coconino forest to the Grand Canyon Camp, at Tolfree. Mr. Tolfree is the genial host who, as it is now supper time, will lead you to where you shall inaugurate your season of beatific rest and sightseeing with a most refreshing and toothsome repast.[175]

There are several interesting things about Neeff's account. The night before he went to the Canyon, he stayed at the Bank Hotel, and the stage stopped at the hotel in the morning to pick up traveler-guests who were staying there. This practice may have given rise to the oft-stated but erroneous belief that the Bank Hotel was the terminus of the stage line. Once underway, the first stage stop was at Little Spring. In previous years, the stage had made its first stop at the Dillman Ranch, next to Fern Mountain, in the Hart Prairie area, a ranch owned by Gus Dillman Freudenberger and his wife Lina. (The Freudenberger name was so hard for Flagstaff residents to handle that the German immigrants had become used to calling themselves Dillman). Perhaps Thurber changed the location of the first relay station when he took over the line from Wilcox. We have found nothing to make the date of the changeover explicit, but as Neeff makes clear, the first stop was not at the Dillman Ranch in 1895.[176] His comment that lunch at East Cedar was served by Mrs. Klostermeyer is also interesting. Sharlot Hall mentioned passing the Klostermeyer place just before reaching East Cedar Ranch in her 1893 trip. By our reckoning, the Klostermeyer ranch was about three miles by wagon road from the East Cedar stage stop. William Klostermeyer, who homesteaded the ranch, was a wool grower known as Missouri Bill, a tempestuous man who was murdered in May 1895.[177] Neeff's driver was Bob Ferguson, who was also mentioned by Edith S. Tupper.[178]

Edith Sessions Tupper wrote an account of her trip, which she took in July 1895. It is amusing to note that, while the English tourist-writer a few days earlier had found Flagstaff to be, "a remarkably pretty little town...and the only place of any note we encountered after leaving Albuquerque...," Ms. Tupper had a contrary opinion:

It was a glorious July morning when the writer left the Pullman sleeper on the Santa Fe route at Flagstaff, Arizona. Flagstaff is a typical frontier town, rough and tumble in atmosphere, architecturally ugly, filled with cowboys and lumbermen. Its main street is lined with saloons and faro rooms and crowded with toughs and drunken men. It is a town to leave as quickly as possible, and, therefore, we were not slow in making our arrangements to get away to the canyon. The manager of the stage line is an accommodating man, and will send tourists on at almost any hour of the day or night.

Fortunate, indeed, was the writer to have the box seat with Robert Ferguson,[179] driver...who drives a stage in summer and spends the winters mining in the canyon. He was a pack outfitter in Salt Lake

City when Powell was getting ready to start on his expedition, and had the honor of fitting out a pack train for the explorers.... He laid out a trail known as the 'Bright Angel Trail....

There are three relays on this ride, and at noon a stop is made at Cedar Ranch for dinner, a lonely cabin situated at the foot of a range of desolate mountains. Before its doors stretches an interminable plain of sand and cacti. No greater or more mournful solitude could be imagined. Here a widow [the newly-widowed Lora Klostermeyer, no doubt] lives with her two little girls and a young lad for company.

Nothing relieves the monotony of the scene until about four o'clock, when the road enters the Coconino Forest.

The stage goes thundering down a hill, and draws up before a log cabin surrounded by a dozen or more tents. In front of the cabin, on a wooden bench, sits a sturdy man of about fifty, whose tawny hair and beard are liberally sprinkled with gray. He wears a suit of brown velveteen and a great flapping sombrero; and the stage driver says, with a great flourish of his whip: "Ladies and gentlemen, allow me to present to you Captain John Hance, who has lived here for the last twelve or fifteen years, and who knows more about the canyon than any man living...."

You constantly hear references to "Hance's trail," and "Hance's new trail," "Hance's old trail," "Hance's Peak," and "Hance's cabin," until you wonder if John Hance owns the Grand Canyon....

In summer Hance lives in a log cabin, hanging on the very rim of the cañon, about a mile from the camp proper. It is the neatest, cleanest place you can imagine. The walls are papered with pictures and lithographs of Buffalo Bill in every pose he ever struck. "Bill Cody!" says Hance. "Shucks! I knew him long before he took to play actin'." Hance does all his own work, and every morning his floor is scrubbed and his stove blackened until they shine and glow. Near his cabin is the corral where he keeps his pack horses which take the trail into the canyon and carry down tourists and provisions. Hance charges twelve dollars a day for his services as guide, philosopher and friend on these excursions. In winter he goes down and lives in the canyon in another log cabin close to the river. "Many's the time I hain't heard a human voice for six months," he tells you. "What do I do to amuse myself? I read the almanac over an' over, from the front to the back, then back again, and sometimes I sing hymns."

After having been presented to this King of the Canyon you register in the log cabin which is a combination hotel office and storehouse for tinned meats and vegetables, hams and bacon. Then you are shown to your tent, which is a most comfortable affair. The wooden floors are covered with Navajo blankets for rugs, the iron bedsteads have excellent mattresses and plenty of clean furnishings....

The bell is ringing for supper in the dining tent, down there in the hollow, close under the hill....

The descent into the canyon is a feat only to be undertaken by those who possess great power of endurance and the steadiest of nerves. The Hance trail, which is the one most in use, begins about a mile from the camp.... The guide himself is an imposing figure as he leads the way.[180] [This description matches the Old Hance Trail, not the Red Canyon Trail].

Business was so brisk in the summer of 1895 that Thurber had to cast aside his tri-weekly schedule and run coaches every day.[181] (although it is probable that he observed Sunday as a day of rest). This no doubt meant increasing the number of horses and mules, and perhaps augmenting his

Hance at his cabin, ready for the trail

Man at Sunset Point, also known as Lookout Point and Observation Point. This was the first view of the Canyon for travelers on the stage line

The authors re-create the above scene, Sherry taking the photo, Richard standing at the point. The view from the point is stunning

staff of drivers. Thurber announced that he was ready at all times to take fifty people to the Canyon and with three days' notice could take twice that amount.[182] The *Sun* noted that the tourist trade was so active that the Bank hotel fed seventy-one people one night in June.[183]

Tourism was not the only thing bringing people to the Grand Canyon in 1895, for there was much excitement about mining. Prospectors were going to the Canyon in droves and exciting rumors filled the air. This led the *Sun* to opine,

Stoddard's Lectures

This photograph shows the outgoing and incoming stages meeting at East Cedar Ranch, the midway point. Heavy business caused Thurber to run daily stages in 1895, 1896, 1897 and 1899, even though the advertising mentioned only a tri-weekly schedule

There is no doubt but what the richest mines in the world are located in the Grand Canyon. Mining men are commencing to realize this and some of the biggest syndicates in the country are making preparations to locate there. It is the only undeveloped country in the United States where all kinds of mineral are certain to be found and the men who cover the field now are certain to reap fortunes.[184]

This double-pull of tourism and mining generated another railroad effort, and in the early part of 1895, there was much talk about a new proposed line, the name of which tells the story, The Durango, Flagstaff & San Diego. It was the brainchild of Wilson Hamilton, who appeared in Flagstaff and enlisted the support of some prominent citizens, including David Babbitt and D. M. Riordan.[185] One of the organizers was Thomas Bullock, the man behind the ill-fated Prescott & Arizona Central, which had run from Seligman to Prescott.[186] Money was spent, surveys were made, and the press was informed that progress was rapid and certain.[187] Like all other prospects before it, this railroad, though touted as a "sure thing," came to nought, and may have been a swindle by Hamilton.

Hard on the heels of this failed venture came another railroad proposal, this time for an electric train, when the Flagstaff & Canyon railroad was incorporated in June.[188] Spearheading the venture was J. A. Fleming. He made a proposal to Flagstaff investors: if they would grade twenty miles of the line, which would cost $20,000, secure the right of way, and built a terminal, he would give them $40,000 worth of stock in his railroad.[189] Townspeople raised $15,000. Fleming spent $5,000 of his own money and hired surveyors to stake out the line and make maps; but this proposal, like all the others, failed.[190]

In August 1895 a regrettable record was set when the first tourist fatality was recorded at the Grand Canyon. A young Yale student was killed by lightning while out hiking along the Rim from Thurber's Camp.[191]

The stage line's season ended November 1 in 1895, although Thurber told the traveling public that he would take special hires to the Canyon if proper arrangements were made ahead of time, weather permitting.[192] Thurber then took some of his horses and wagons to Yucca, Arizona, where he spent the winter doing grading work for the Atlantic & Pacific Railroad and running a stage service to a nearby mine.[193, 194]

In October 1895 the *Sun* carried a story that L. H. Tolfree and John Hance had gone to Los Angeles together.[195] Perhaps they were carrying on negotiations for the business transaction that occurred soon afterwards, for by means of a Deed dated November 1, 1895, J. W. Thurber, L. H. Tolfree and I. F. "Ike" Wheeler bought John Hance's trail business.

The transaction is confusing, so a bit of explanation may be in order. Hance had no title to the land where Hance Camp was located, merely squatter's rights. These rights allowed him nothing more than the bare opportunity to perfect a homestead, and—if he followed all the rules and things went well—get a Patent.[196] By law, homestead rights were non-transferable, and Hance could not sell them to Thurber and his associates.[197] The complete text of the description of the property transferred by the Deed is as follows:[198]

> That certain trail known as the Hance Trail. Commencing at a point on the rim about one-half mile east of the Grand Canyon Hotel and at the Hance Cabin, run thence to the Colorado River, together with that certain spring and rock cabin known as the Hance Spring and Rock Cabin, beside the trail about three miles from the start. All personal property used in connection with the said trail and in the operation, to-wit:
>
> > 6 mules: Beck, Biddy, Kate, Jim, Kitty and Steve
> > 6 horses: Sabine, George, Aleck, Nig, Buck, Gray Mare Kitty
> > 8 men's saddles
> > 1 side saddle
> > 9 bridles
> > 9 saddle blankets
>
> Buyers will use the trail and equipment in connection with the Grand Canyon Hotel and in the business of renting the trail and guiding visitors. Price $1500.00. Hance will not "at any time hereafter" engage in the business of guide, at any point within thirty miles of said Grand Canyon Hotel. Hance grants an easement across his pasture for trailhead access and the right to graze the animals in his pasture.
>
> Sale also includes his 1/4 interest in The Red Canyon Trail about one mile east of the Hance Trail and in which I am 1/4 owner. The Red Canyon Trail shall not be used for other than mining purposes. I will prevent Red Canyon Trail being used by tourists.

The gist of this transaction was that Hance was out of the tourist business at the Grand Canyon. The fact that Hance only gave the buyers an easement across the pasture indicated that he intended to retain his possessory rights to the land, and in fact, years later, Hance filed a new Homestead notice on the property—with a somewhat different description—and eventually received a Patent for it on February 25, 1907.[199]

Following their purchase, Thurber and his associates built an additional wooden building on the Camp property, a log structure that was used as a kitchen and dining room. Thurber and his partners then changed the name of Hance's Camp to the Grand Canyon Hotel, although it was also known as Thurber's Camp, or the Canyon Camp and other names.[200]

One wonders why Hance would have agreed to sell his trails and equipment and stop acting as a trail guide. Most of his livelihood at the time seems to have depended on the income he received from guiding, rather than from his mining interests. By 1895 Hance had so established his reputation as a Canyon fixture that seeing him and listening to his tall tales were considered to be an essential part of the Grand Canyon experience. His reputation was a valuable right, not to be abandoned lightly.

The fact that Thurber and his associates bought the old and new trails from Hance is interesting. It has been stated by a knowledgeable historian that the Old Hance Trail was wiped out by a rock slide in 1894.[201] Comments made in Hance's Guest Book show that tourists were using the new—Red Canyon—trail in the fall of 1894. For example, the Fancher family wrote: "We all went down the new trail on September 21st to the river...riding horseback nearly all the way." In a similar vein, the Meguire party noted on October 7, 1894, "Visited Grand Cañon via Hance's new trail." And D. K. Fitzhugh on November 12, 1894, wrote, "Went to river via Hance's New Trail." There are no references to a new trail earlier than September 1894.[202]

If it be true that the Old Hance Trail was wiped out in 1894, then it is

GCM 5114

The 1895 additions to Hance's Camp, by now called Thurber's Camp. The big log structure was a kitchen-dining room. The wing on the back of the building contained living quarters for the managers. Note that the guests are still living in tents

GCM 4500

Some time later a porch was added to the dining hall

GCM 16247

Fully developed. Note that the porch has been widened and the roof line above it is different. The old cabin seems very rustic, even primitive

34

4

Stoddard's Lectures

Starting down the Hance Trail

hard to understand why Thurber and his partners would buy the trail from Hance in November 1895. Harvey Butchart, dean of Grand Canyon hikers, stated that he hiked the Old Hance Trail (probably in the 1950s or 1960s) and found the names and dates of hikers carved on a canyon wall far down the trail, the inscribed dates running from 1885 to 1895, suggesting that the trail was still being used in 1895.[203] It may have been in use years later, because the *Coconino Sun* reported in 1901:

> The old Hance and Red Canyon trails are not so much used as formerly, but both are good, and the old Hance trail is especially picturesque.[204]

The *Sun* also reported in 1901 that Hance built another trail, the Rim Trail

> The trip along the rim to Moran and Bissell points over the trail recently constructed by Captain John Hance, is especially recommended, as it undoubtedly affords the finest series of views of the Canyon to be had from the rim....[205]

We believe that the Rim Trail ran along the top of the Rim, but there is some authority that it ran below the Rim, connecting the New and Old Hance Trails.[206] The matter seems unresolved, tantalizingly uncertain.

As to the Red Canyon trail, the language of the 1895 Deed recites that Hance owned a one-quarter interest in it. As we have already seen, the *Coconino Sun* carried an article in 1891 to the effect that McClure, Marshall, Ashurst and Frier were building the trail. It is not clear how Hance acquired a one-quarter interest in it. Hance often claimed that he built the trail by himself, but the evidence suggests that this statement was another of his famous fabrications.[207]

Thurber spent the winter of 1895-96 performing a grading contract for the Atlantic & Pacific in the Western Arizona desert, near Yucca, to which he moved horses, wagons, scrapers and other equipment. His job was to widen the roadbed.[208] After this was finished, he did work in California for the Santa Fe Pacific Railroad.[209] He also ran a stage line from Yucca to a mining district.[210]

1896

J. W. Thurber was a busy fellow early in the year 1896. He sold his stage line at Yucca,[211] and dissolved his logging company partnership with T. H. Carter, taking over the entire operation.[212]

The dream of an electric railroad from Flagstaff to the Grand Canyon, which had been left hanging over the winter, apparently died, but its promoter, J. A. Fleming still had ambitions, and he re-entered the field in 1896 with a new proposal, for a railroad called the Globe, Flagstaff & Canyon, into which he sank a considerable portion of his own money for a survey.[213]

The stage line began taking passengers to the Canyon on April 1 in 1896, still under the management of James W. Thurber, who reported that he could provide superb rides in two fine Concord coaches as well as a number of smaller vehicles. He also told the traveling public of the improved amenities at Thurber's Camp:

> Among the additional accommodations which have been made, a new hotel has been built. The building is of logs, 40 x 60 feet, and contains a dining and sitting room and a kitchen.[214]

Thurber was referring to the log building added to Thurber's Camp to supplement Hance's original log cabin, though it seems that describing it as a "hotel" was stretching the facts. Guests would continue to sleep in tents. In Flagstaff, Thurber improved the stage line's office at the railroad depot and hung out a sign displaying the timetable, so that train passengers could see it.[215]

At the beginning of 1896 the only tourism activity in the vicinity of today's Grand Canyon Village was the little operation of Sanford Rowe at Rowe Well. Rowe had found water at the site, one of the very few places near the Rim where there is any, and in 1892 had bought the stage line that William Bass had been running from Williams to Bass Camp, using it to take tourists instead to a tent camp that he set up at Rowe Well, west of today's Village. He then secured permission from the Cameron brothers and Pete Berry to take tourists down the Bright Angel Trail, the trailhead for which was about three miles away from his tourist camp.[216] He also built a road to Rowe Point, later called Hopi Point.

Grand Canyon of Arizona

Original Bright Angel Hotel

For reasons that we have been unable to find, Thurber decided to build a hotel near the head of the Bright Angel Trail in 1896. Since the land was in the Grand Canyon Forest Reserve, created in 1893, he obtained a permit from "Washington,"[217] but did not get a special use permit or any other ownership or possessory rights to the property on which the hotel was to be built.[218] His specifications for the building were, "Log House 24 x 32 and log kitchen 12 x 14 to be built at Grand Cañon. Must be completed by May 1, 1896."[219] It contained eight guest rooms.[220] Thurber called his inn the Bright Angel Hotel, the first structure at today's Village.[221] He supplemented the few rooms in the log building with tents.[222]

Anyone with hotel facilities near the Bright Angel Trail would have wanted trail privileges, and it is likely that Thurber worked out an arrangement with the Camerons and Berry, but the authors have seen no records to prove the truth of this surmise. (Pete Berry had filed a Toll Road Certificate on the Bright Angel Trail in his name only in 1891,[223] but he spent no time at Bright Angel, leaving it to the Cameron brothers to operate the trail and the mining activities there, while he attended to the operations at Grandview, and in time he and the others would sell their interests so that Ralph Cameron would end up as sole owner).

America, Her Grandeur and Her Beauty

Bright Angel Hotel, detail

Thurber kept a guest register for the Bright Angel Hotel that is now in the archives of the Museum of Northern Arizona.[224] The register shows a fair amount of trade in 1896, although it is not clear why Thurber wanted a second hotel so far away from his base camp at the end of the stage road. Perhaps some of the tourists who came from Williams wanted better accommodations than Rowe could deliver at Rowe Well, and some who came from Flagstaff wanted better than they found at Thurber's Camp. Perhaps travelers wanted to see more of the Canyon. Perhaps it was, in part, a response to increasing competition from Pete Berry at the Grandview, as Berry had been fixing up and increasing the size of his hostelry there from year to year, and since 1895 had been calling it a hotel.[225]

To link his tourist lodgings together, Thurber constructed a road from Thurber's Camp, running about fourteen miles through Long Jim and Shoski Canyons, to Bright Angel.[226] This road was used until 1929 as the main road east from the Village.[227] The construction of this road, with hotels owned by Thurber at each end, gave Thurber a dominant position in tourism at the Canyon.

Hotel construction was taking place in Flagstaff, too. The *Sun* carried a story in June 1896 that the David Babbitt building would be turned into a hotel. This building was a two-story wooden structure located on the south-

Stoddard's Lectures

Entering the caves was not easy

MNA MS 26-5a

Tourists in the Crystal Caves help themselves to chunks of stalactite as souvenirs

MNA MS 26-36b

The porch of the Grandview Hotel was littered with left-behind souvenirs from the caves

west corner of Aspen Avenue and San Francisco Street. The new hostelry was called the Grand Canyon Hotel,[228] and it opened for business on July 1, 1896, just in time to enjoy the high point of the tourist season.[229] (Oscar LeBarron, its manager, had an unusual connection to Grand Canyon tourism: the woman he would marry in November 1896 was the widow Lora Klostermeyer, who had run the stage stop at East Cedar Ranch). LeBarron had a partner in the hotel enterprise, none other than J. W. Thurber. It seemed that Thurber was engaged in a program of covering the tourist business from all angles, with hotels at Flagstaff, Thurber's Camp and the Bright Angel—together with a stage line to link them together.[230]

The premier Flagstaff inn was still the Bank Hotel, but it was doing poorly in 1896. In April its manager, T. J. Coalter, announced that due to the depression that was still dampening business as a result of the Panic of '93, he was cutting his rates.[231] In November 1896, Coalter leased the hotel to L. H. Tolfree, who was to take over the place on December 1, 1896, when Coalter's lease expired.[232] After Tolfree took over the lodging, he started calling it the New Bank Hotel.[233] Tolfree cut his ties with the Grand Canyon-Flagstaff Stage Line at the end of the 1896 season, moved to Flagstaff, and devoted his full time to the New Bank Hotel. He probably dissolved his business associations with Thurber, such as the co-ownership of the usage rights to the Hance Trail, though we were unable to find any records to this effect.

The former operator of the Grand Canyon Stage Line, E. S. Wilcox, suffered a big loss in April 1896 when his Grand Canyon Livery Stable on the west side of north Leroux Street in Flagstaff burned to the ground. The fire spread to adjacent buildings, causing tremendous devastation and nearly burning to death three prisoners trapped in the town jail, who were rescued at the last minute.[234]

As if the Grand Canyon were not already scenic enough, it was announced in May 1896 that wonderful caves had been discovered there, full of stalactites and stalagmites, something else for visitors to see. These caves were below Horseshoe Mesa, and could be reached by the Grandview Trail.[235] This scenic attraction would bring more visitors to the Canyon, and gave some advantage to Pete Berry, as the caves could be reached only by his trail, not the Red Canyon Trail controlled by Thurber. The *Sun* reported in late July 1896 that travel over the Grandview Trail had been good over the previous ten days, with fifty-one tourists making the trip, many attracted by news of the caves.[236] Berry and Cameron were operating the Last Chance Mine full tilt in 1896 as well as trying to develop their tourism business.[237]

The fact that reliable transportation to the Grand Canyon was available from Flagstaff seemed to reach out in ever-widening circles. The famous Thomas Cook Travel Agency of London started booking trips to the Canyon, with its first group of customers making the journey in the summer of 1896, guided by George Wharton James, an author and early popularizer of the Grand Canyon, who spent much time at the Canyon and wrote several books about it.[238]

The informality with which ownership rights in Grand Canyon property was handled in the early days has caused trouble not only for historians, but seemed to plague the pioneers as well. On November 1, 1895, Thurber, Tolfree and Wheeler had purchased from John Hance the right to use his trails, including Hance's self-stated one-quarter interest in the Red Canyon Trail. In September 1896, Thurber (in his name only, with no mention of Tolfree and Wheeler) apparently decided that there were some loose ends in his rights in the Red Canyon Trail, because he sought and obtained a Deed from C. H. McClure, John Marshall and T. C. Frier for,

> ...a three-fifths interest in trail in Grand Canyon Mining District about three-quarters mile east of John Hance Trail. Grantors may use the trail for mining purposes only.[239]

Anyone doing simple arithmetic would wonder how the fractions added up: how to reconcile the difference between Hance's one-fourth and the three-fifths interests of the McClure group. Converting these fractions to percentages, they would produce a sum of eighty-five percent, leaving fifteen percent floating around unaccounted for. It is likely that the parties believed that the result of the two transactions was that J. W. Thurber owned all of the Red Canyon Trail, subject only to the right of the miners to use it for mining purposes.

In October 1896, perhaps encouraged by the increase of tourism caused by the announcement of the cave discovery, Pete Berry at Grandview began the construction of an honest-to-goodness hotel, to replace his existing structure that had grown like Topsy from a simple mine shack. He wrote his son on October 13, 1896, "I am getting out logs to build a house 24 feet wide by 54 feet long 2 story, for a hotel. But I do not expect to have it finished until spring."[240]

Munk, Arizona Sketches

The Grandview Hotel, as enlarged in 1896. Note that it, too, used tents to handle overflow

John Hance got back into the guide business in 1896. On November 5, 1896, J. W. Thurber signed a Release, canceling Hance's covenant not to compete that had been created in the Deed signed in November 1895.[241] No reason for the release was given on the face of the document and we have been unable to locate any information elsewhere to show why Thurber relieved Hance of the restriction. One surmises that having Hance act as a guide was good for both parties. The Deed signed by Hance in 1895 had run in favor of Thurber, L. H. Tolfree and I. F. Wheeler. The Release, signed a year later, was executed only by Thurber, implying that whatever association had existed among Thurber, Tolfree and Wheeler had been dissolved, with Thurber as the sole surviving owner of the group's interests. Tolfree's withdrawal is explained by his taking over the New Bank Hotel in Flagstaff.[242]

The bankruptcy proceedings that had tied up the workings of the Atlantic & Pacific Railroad for many months ended in 1896, with a successor line, the Santa Fe Pacific, emerging.[243]

Thurber spent the winter of 1896-97 at work on a contract to haul timbers, ore and supplies for mines in the White Hills District near Kingman, Arizona.[244] He seems to have been a tireless worker, and it made good sense to keep his animals productive. In January 1897 he shipped teams, wagons and freighting outfits from Flagstaff to Kingman, "putting on three or four eight-horse teams."[245] A week later he shipped over several more teams.[246] That adds up to a lot of horses.

1897

As 1897 opened, the air was full of excitement about new mineral discoveries in and around the Grand Canyon. The well-known W. O. "Buckey" O'Neill of Prescott, one of the locators and promoters of these claims, began enlisting the support of wealthy Eastern men to bond the properties, the first step in a development program that was designed to include the construction of the long-desired railroad to the Grand Canyon.[247] O'Neill's main interest was in recently located copper discoveries at Anita, south of the Canyon, and after much effort, he was able to convince Eastern capitalists to pump money into the development of the mines, including a railroad. The people of Flagstaff still assumed that this—

Ad for the ill-fated Grand Canon Hotel

James E. Babbitt

The stage line's new office in the Babbitt Building in downtown Flagstaff. Gold lettering on the four windows above the door is visible. It read "Grand Cañon Stage Office." In the foreground, left, is the rubble from the burnt Grand Canyon Hotel, dating this photo as September or October 1897

Sherry G. Mangum

The location of the stage coach office today. James E. Babbitt, a historian, has restored the lettering to the windows where the office was located

or any other—railroad to the Grand Canyon would have its terminus in their town.[248]

Just before the tourist season began, in March 1897, J. W. Thurber dissolved his partnership with Oscar LeBarron in the Grand Canyon Hotel in Flagstaff, leaving the enterprise in the hands of LeBarron.[249] LeBarron, who was also engaged in farming and sheep ranching, made improvements to the hotel and had it in first-class operating condition by the time the tourist season opened.

Thurber began running the Grand Canyon-Flagstaff Stage Line about the first of April in 1897.[250] In addition to his small facility at the railroad depot, he opened an office in the Babbitt Building on the northwest corner of San Francisco Street and Aspen Avenue. The suite was upstairs, above the main entrance on the corner, and contained a waiting room, information bureau and office.[251] Out the window to the south, Thurber could look directly at the Grand Canyon Hotel across Aspen Avenue.

Thurber hired George K. Woods, stationed in the new Flagstaff headquarters, as the general manager of the line,[252] then arranged to run daily stages to take care of the anticipated big demand, with Howard Marine as one of his drivers.[253] Thurber himself moved to the Canyon with his family to spend the summer at the Bright Angel Hotel.[254] Later he hired a manager for the dining room at the hotel, C. A. Hageman, who came from Los Angeles to take the position.[255] At the time, Thurber was still actively engaged in his work freighting mining supplies at White Hills in Western Arizona.[256]

At the Canyon Pete Berry was hard at work building the new Grandview Hotel, and the *Sun* reported that the firm of Berry and Cameron would be operating both mining and tourism businesses in 1897. By late April the hotel was still not quite ready, but would be open soon, using—in part—lumber that was milled at the site.[257, 258] Although the newspaper might have announced that Berry would be running both the mine and the hotel, a letter from Ralph Cameron (who was Sheriff of Coconino County and had to spend most of his time in Flagstaff, the county seat) suggests that the men were really going to concentrate on tourism only—with no mining—that year. Cameron wrote Berry on April 20, 1897:

> I will send some bedding and cots out just as soon as I can get my wagon, will send some bedding by the team tomorrow, also some groceries. I dont think it best for us to expend much money, as I am in H— hole now paying bills. However, I have them all fixed up. I dont think it wise for us to move on the mine, only to do the assessment work and that we can do on the trail.[259]

Cameron's mention of "assessment work" was a reference to a provision in the mining laws—designed to weed out fraudulent or worthless claims—that required locators of a mine to carry out annual development work and file an Affidavit of Labor Performed with the County Recorder in order to maintain the validity of a claim. Cameron was evading the spirit of the law but meeting its letter by suggesting that their assessment work be done on the Grandview Trail even though the partners' real purpose would be to use the trail for tourism rather than mining.[260] Cameron added,

> I think we can make a good deal of money out of the trail and pasture and water this season as the RR people have advertised more than ever and they are expending lots of money fixing up the track.[261]

At Thurber's Camp, the post office that had been known as Tolfree was closed because L. H. Tolfree was no longer part of the enterprise. A new post office named Tourist was created in its place, with John Hance as postmaster.[262]

Will Hochderffer replaced the widow Klostermeyer as the manager of the East Cedar Ranch Station. He and his family moved to the isolated site to spend the tourist season there.[263]

Business started off well for the Grand Canyon Stage Line in 1897. It was reported in May that Thurber was so busy that he sent out three coaches in one day, a six-horse, a four and a two, and that he was expecting a special charter party of forty tourists from Boston.[264] Some of the trips were arranged for variety, taking the eastern route on the way out to the Canyon and the westerly route on the way back to Flagstaff.[265] Thurber was using both horses and mules to pull the coaches, "as the country required."[266]

One tourist, E. E. See, brother of a Lowell Observatory astronomer, took the stage trip in May 1897 and wrote an account of his experience that was published in the Flagstaff newspaper. One of his fellow passengers on the journey was none other than John Hance, who was taking the coach to the Canyon. Mr. See reported that Hance could not only tell stories, but was the best singer of the bunch, with a very good voice, exceeding in quality even the voices of the women.[267] At Cedar Ranch, while See was eating lunch, the stage from the Canyon to Flagstaff pulled in, proof that Thurber was indeed running daily stages, with two-way traffic, early in the 1897 season, as he had foretold.

The lingering depression that had been caused by the Panic of '93 was all but forgotten in the spring of 1897. Flagstaff's newspaper, the *Flagstaff Sun-Democrat*[268], said:

> Boom times are reported. Much excitement about mining around here. Sheep and cattle are in good condition and prices are high. The largest planting ever of potatoes this year. The saw mills of Greenlaw and Arizona Lumber are running full time. Travel to the Grand Canyon of the Colorado is much better than for years, in fact it never was so bright.

The proprietors of the New Bank and Grand Canyon Hotels say tourist business is greater than it ever has been at this time of year before. The Stage line to the Grand Canyon is doing a big business, and tourists and sightseers as well as health seekers are arriving on every train.[269]

The *Phoenix Gazette* reported that conditions were excellent in Flagstaff, describing the situation in general and then homing in on the stagecoach:

> Every other day the mammoth stages ply between Flagstaff and the Grand Canyon, the average cost for the round trip being about $15, not including hotel bills. The first class hotels charge but $2.50 per day. The road from Flagstaff to the Canyon is an excellent one, easily made by wheel [bicycle], and annually there is a Territorial run made from the city to the Canyon.[270]

By June 1897, G. K. Woods, the new manager of the stage line, was reporting that it was enjoying its best year ever.[271] The Flagstaff newspa-

GRAND CANYON STAGE LINE

—FROM—

FLAGSTAFF, ARIZONA,

—TO—

Grand Canyon of the Colorado River.

Round Trip Tickets, Flagstaff to Canyon, $15.00.

Hotel Rates at the Canyon, $3.00 per Day.

J. W. THURBER, Proprietor.

FOUR AND SIX HORSE COACHES leave Flagstaff Mondays, Wednesdays and Fridays, 7 a. m.; 30 minutes' stop at Cedar Springs for Dinner. Return Tuesdays, Thursdays and Saturdays. Excellent Hotel accommodations at Canyon in connection with Stage Line.

READY FOR THE CANYON AND OTHER POINTS OF INTEREST.

Horses, Vehicles, Competent Drivers and Guides furnished at reasonable rates. Special attention given to Tourists wishing to visit any point of interest, such as

GRAND CANYON OF THE COLORADO RIVER—Sixty-five miles. Scenery indescribable.
CATARACT CANYON—Sixty-five miles. The abode of the Supai Indians. Can be entered only on horseback.
NATURAL BRIDGE—Seventy-five miles. Arch, 250 feet; width, 500; height, 275 feet.
MONTEZUMA WELL AND CASTLE—Fifty miles. Point of great interest.
OAK CREEK CANYON—Seventeen miles. Good trout fishing.
THE ICE CAVES—Nine miles. A natural cold storage.
WALNUT CANYON—Eight miles. The home of the Cliff Dwellers, a pre-historic race of four or more hundred years ago. Walls of castles perfect.
SUNSET MOUNTAIN—Ten miles. An extinct volcano, supposed to have been active four hundred years ago.
CAVE DWELLINGS—Eight miles. The home of a pre-historic race.
THE BLACK CRATER—Fifteen miles. In the center of the largest lava beds in the world.
SAN FRANCISCO PEAKS—Thirteen miles. With an altitude of 14,000 feet. Snow-capped most of the year. From the top, with a good glass, one can see almost one-third of the Territory.
THE MOQUI VILLAGE—Seventy-five miles. The home of the Snake Dance.

For further information address,

G. K. WOODS, General Manager,

Flagstaff, Arizona.

Thurber's ad, 1897. This could have depicted a busy day or he might have been posing for the photo with his best teams and running rigs. The little stage office is visible to the left of the depot.

per, musing on the tourism boom, printed a prophetic pronouncement, in which the editor predicted: "Should a railroad ever be built to the Grand Canyon, it will become one of the greatest resorts in America."[272]

The stagecoach road (probably the Western Route) was improved in the summer of 1897. According to the newspaper:

> Road overseer Anderson has just completed the work of clearing out the malapai that studded a long stretch of the road to the Grand Canyon, and that thoroughfare is now as smooth as a boulevard.[273]

For the first time, a woman made the bicycle trip from Flagstaff to the Canyon in 1897.[274] This groundbreaking trip is covered more fully in this book's chapter on bicycle travel.

A long-time resident of Flagstaff, W. H. Carroll, attempted to cash in on the tourist trade by adding another level to his restaurant building at 18 N. San Francisco Street, calling the upper story the Carrollton Hotel. It was ready for business in July 1897, competing with the New Bank Hotel and the Grand Canyon Hotel.[275]

A West Coast travel writer took the stagecoach in the 1897 season and described the trip for readers:

> On the train, the worst desert is passed over during the night, so that one awakens in the pines. Breakfast is served at Williams, and at 9:45 the train pulls into Flagstaff.... It is impossible to push directly on, for the train does not get in until 9:45 a.m., and the stage leaves at 7 o'clock sharp....[276]

> To people who enjoy dashing along behind spirited horses through the keen, sparkling air and over a hard, smooth road, the prospect of a railroad to the Grand Canyon brings but little pleasure. If ever a stage road should survive, to bring memories of the merry coaching days of old, it is this line between Flagstaff and the Grand Canyon....

> Cedar Ranch and its log house are reached about luncheon time, and as it is also time for a walk,[277] the horses take a rest while the passengers hunt for queer specimens of petrified wood which abound in these forests....[278]

> There are three horse relays at intervals of about 20 miles. After a sharp descent into a picturesque little gorge, the stage pulls up at Camp Thurber, a comfortable permanent camp, where it is possible to obtain a hearty meal and a good bed. It is a village of tents, but each tent is floored and furnished like the quarters of a field officer so there is little chance for roughing it in any way. Here at Camp Thurber are well trained saddle horses, donkeys and guides for exploring the Grand Canyon. It is possible to return by the stage next day.[279]

Another writer described the tent camp as:

> ...a city of tents, with the proverbial main street, and following the Eastern procedure, their numbers ran odd on one side, and even on the other, with avenues crossing at right angles.[280]

This same writer, George B. Reese, was greatly pleased with the manager of the camp, a young man named J. S. Clayton, for whom he predicted a bright future.[281] Nothing more is known about Clayton nor whether he fulfilled the promise shown at the Camp that summer.

As if Thurber were not busy enough with his stage line, hotels and contracting business in 1897, the Flagstaff newspaper mentioned that he was also engaged in another occupation:

> James W. Thurber is not only a stage manager, but he is also somewhat of a granger. He is having over one hundred acres put in grain in the valley above the T. F. McMillon farm.[282]

The Carrollton Hotel

Thurber seems to have finished his freighting job for the mines near Kingman in the summer of 1897, but picked up another big contract, this time for the Santa Fe Railroad, immediately afterwards. The newspaper gave the information in July that:

> J. W. Thurber, who has a contract with the railroad at Seligman, shipped a car load of horses Tuesday, in charge of E. R. Bayless, to assist in carrying on the work at the dam at the above named town.[283]

The contract was a large one, for the newspaper later stated:

> J. W. Thurber shipped on Sunday six teams to Seligman where he has a contract with the Santa Fe railroad on the new dam being built there. This makes a total of 28 teams that Mr. Thurber has at Seligman.[284] [The number of animals was reduced a bit later when lightning struck his construction camp at Seligman and killed two mules. Five men were hit, but none suffered lasting injury].[285]

The area where Thurber had his farm

Thurber obtained yet another contract toward the end of the summer, this time to do work on the grading for the construction of the tie-pickling plant at Bellemont. Again, this work was performed for the Santa Fe Railroad.[286]

Anyone who was interested in the Grand Canyon noticed that the Santa Fe & Grand Canyon Railroad Company was incorporated on July 31, 1897. Its name was misleading, as the railroad was a brand-new one and had nothing to do with the Santa Fe Pacific or any of its divisions. The Santa Fe & Grand Canyon Railroad Co. was a startup operation financed by Lombard, Goode & Company whose intention was to build a railroad from a point on the Santa Fe line—either Williams or Flagstaff—to the Grand Canyon. Flagstaff seemed to have the edge as the site to be chosen.[287] The competition between Flagstaff and Williams for the prize was keen, and as the year went on, it intensified, so that by September it was reported that rivalry between the towns for the railroad connection was "rampant".[288]

The financiers sent out a surveying party to help settle the matter, with the mission of picking the best route, by mapping the route from Williams to the Canyon, then doing the same thing from the Canyon to Flagstaff, a project that would take several weeks. The results would enable the railroad developers to decide which to choose.[289]*The Williams News* accused Flagstaff parties of offering a bonus to the railroad company to induce it to choose their town.[290] While out-and-out bribery is unlikely to have occurred, Flagstaff businessmen did hold a banquet for officials of the proposed railroad at the New Bank Hotel, where they were wined, dined and speechified.[291] The tension between the towns mounted as the survey crew worked its way to the Canyon late in the year and then headed toward Flagstaff.[292] By the end of 1897, the surveyors had still not reached Flagstaff, and the choice was still unresolved.

While all this was going on, officials of the Santa Fe Railroad were quoted as saying that they would like to see a railroad built to the Grand Canyon but that they were not going to put any money into such a venture since they needed to devote all available funds to the improvement of their existing lines.[293] A bit later, the president of the Santa Fe spoke of an electric railroad to the Canyon, something he said was a sure thing for the spring of 1898.[294] There was a later announcement in 1897 of yet another attempt to build a railroad from Flagstaff to the Grand Canyon, this time led by attorney E. E. Ellinwood.[295]

Though tourism played an important part in motivating investors to consider building a railroad to the Grand Canyon, the real driving force was the then feverish interest in mining. In 1897, the great Klondike Gold Rush was on, and some Arizona boosters predicted that the Grand Canyon mines had the potential to become the next Klondike.[296]

In mid-September 1897 fire consumed the Grand Canyon Hotel in Flagstaff.[297] This left Lyman Tolfree, at the New Bank Hotel, sitting pretty, with the best place in town, as his hostelry was a definite cut above the Carrollton Hotel, his only remaining competitor.[298]

A professional travel-writer and lecturer, John Stoddard, took the Grand Canyon-Flagstaff Stage Line in September 1897. A few of his published remarks are set out:

> One glorious September morning, leaving our train at Flagstaff,[299] we started in stage-coaches for a drive of sixty-five miles to the Grand Cañon. I had looked forward to this drive with some misgiving, dreading the heat of the sun, and the dust and sand which I had supposed we should encounter; but to my astonishment and delight it was a thoroughly enjoyable experience. It was only eleven hours in duration, and not only was most of the route level, but two-thirds of it lay through a section of beautifully rolling land, diversified with open glades and thousands upon thousands of tall pines and cedars entirely free from undergrowth.

Stoddard's Lectures

The Stoddard party at the Flagstaff depot

> About the hour of noon we reached a lunch-station at which the stages, going to and from the Cañon, meet and pass. The structure itself is rather primitive; but a good meal is served to tourists at this wayside halting-place....

One of the passengers in Stoddard's coach was making the journey to determine the advisability of building a railroad from Flagstaff to the Grand Canyon. Stoddard proved himself a poor prophet when he wrote:

> Whether this will be done eventually is not, however, a matter of vital interest to travelers, since the country traversed can easily be made an almost ideal coaching-route; and, with good stages, frequent relays of horses, and a well-appointed lunch-station, a journey thus accomplished would be *preferable* to a trip by rail. [Emphasis added].

> Hance's log cabin serves as a kitchen and dining-room for travelers, and a few guests can even find lodging there; but, until a hotel is built, the principal dormitories must be the tents, which are provided with wooden floors and furnished with tables, chairs, and comfortable beds. This kind of accommodation, however, although excellent for travelers in robust health, is not sufficiently luxurious to attract many tourists. The evident necessity of the place is a commodious, well-kept inn....[300]

Stoddard's observation about stages meeting and passing at the halfway point is notable as evidence that the line was still supporting daily runs in September, near the end of the 1897 season. His comment about how a few guests could find lodging in the new building is interesting, but we found no accounts written by anyone who ever stayed in the building, so the number of rooms and the quality of the accommodations are unknown. All of the surviving written accounts are from travelers who slept in the tents.

Stoddard was right on target in his assessment of the Camp: in order to develop the Grand Canyon into a high-class travel resort that could attract large numbers of visitors, who expected a degree of comfort and cleanliness, a proper hotel must be built. Thurber was no doubt wrestling with this need, and trying to decide what to do about it.

Traffic to the Canyon continued strong throughout the travel-year. The newspaper was happy to report in late September, "No abatement in the travel to the Grand Canyon. This season is a record breaker for visitors."[301]

Thurber must have been feeling prosperous and confident as the 1897 season wore on, for he purchased a house and lots in Flagstaff from Ed Gale and made plans to build a five-room home on the property.[302] [Ed Gale was heavily involved in mining at the Grand Canyon, had worked on the Bright Angel and Grandview Trails and owned an interest in the trails and mines with Berry and the Camerons].

When Thurber closed down for winter on the first of November 1897, he looked back on his best year.[303] He buttoned down his operations at the Canyon, whereupon he returned to Flagstaff, the newspaper noting,

> D. R. Prime and Hugh Bunch left here Tuesday for the Grand Canyon with teams to move the family of J. W. Thurber to town. They will at once move into their new handsome residence which Mr. Thurber has just completed in the west part of our city.[304]

The timing worked out so that Thurber was able to move into his new home in Flagstaff. Thurber then hustled some of his men and equipment to Seligman, where he had twenty-two teams and thirty-five men at work widening the grade of the Santa Fe Railroad from Seligman to Kingman.[305] This seems to have been a large enough contract to occupy his crews over the winter.

1898

J. W. Thurber must have been on cordial terms with the Santa Fe, for he was awarded an additional contract to grade west of Kingman, in the area of Blake, California, in the winter of 1897-1898.[306]

Early in the year, the competition between Flagstaff and Williams to take the prize as terminus for the Grand Canyon railroad was won by Williams, though the *Sun* only grudgingly acknowledged the fact. In February it advised readers that the firm of Lombard, Goode & Co. would not only build the railroad from Williams but would also built a smelter there.[307]

At the beginning of 1898, Thurber renewed his contract with the Santa Fe to run the Grand Canyon-Flagstaff Stage Line. Then he immediately made arrangements for the management of the Bright Angel Hotel.[308] He hired D. R. Prime and his family to take care of the facility at East Cedar Ranch.[309] Thurber re-hired George K. Woods to be the general manager of the stage line, as he had been in 1897. As to the actual running of the stages, the *Flagstaff Gem* reported that,

> J. W. Thurber is making all needful preparations for starting up his stage line from here to the Grand Canyon. He will have everything ready and start up by the 1st of April. He will put on a number of teams, and make tri-weekly trips to the canyon.[310]

The *Sun* gave a report of his preparations for the 1898 season,

> J. W. Thurber has fitted up the Grand Canyon stage line office at the depot. On the south side of the office a neat sign gives the days of the departure and arrival of the stages. The stage line is now ready for business and those intending to visit to the Grand Canyon of the Colorado river will find the accommodations better than ever before.[311]

Flagstaff's other newspaper, the *Gem*, gave additional information about the preparations Thurber was required to make in order to get the stages rolling:

> Half a dozen large tents were shipped here Tuesday for J. W. Thurber's use at the Grand Canyon.

> J. W. Thurber started several wagons and teams out on his Grand Canyon stage line yesterday loaded with grain and equipage

Holmes Travelogues

Burton Holmes's cameraman took this shot in the summer of 1898. It is labeled "On the Main Street." We believe that Holmes himself is on the right and that the other men are stagecoach drivers, although they would have called themselves "teamsters," men who could handle a team preparatory to the starting up of business on his line.[312]

In spite of his plans to open April 1, conditions forced Thurber to delay the opening until April 15.[313]

Thurber must have felt confident and comfortable with his business, with his home and base in Flagstaff, for the newspaper reported that he was building additions to his home and his livery stable.[314]

Holmes Travelogues

John Hance, whom the newspaper called "the only original Grand Canyon guide," bought a house in Flagstaff, from John Marshall, at 113 South San Francisco Street. Marshall, a long-time resident of Flagstaff, had spent much time prospecting and developing mineral properties at the Grand Canyon. It will be remembered that Marshall was one of the group of four who built the Red Canyon Trail in 1891. Hance improved and remodeled Marshall's former house, intending to spend his leisure time in town.[315] Another pal from his mining activities, C. H. McClure, painted the house for him.[316]

In Williams, its townspeople breathlessly awaited the commencement of construction of the railroad to the Canyon. Many businessmen there had invested in the project and were eager to have it completed so that they could receive dividends. They were pleased when, early in March, it was announced that construction of the railroad would soon begin. The editor of the Flagstaff's *Sun*, however—turned cynical by the experience of watching many failed railroad ventures—opined:

Downtown Flagstaff as it appeared to stagecoach travelers in the summer of 1898. This is the block on Front Street (Route 66) running from San Francisco Street to Leroux Street and was known as Saloon Row, Whiskey Row, or similar names. Virtually every business shown here was a saloon. In addition to serving up booze, these places provided other entertainment: gambling and prostitution

> ...it is hoped that the project may be finished. But as so many roads have been started in the direction of the Grand Canyon and abandoned after considerable work was done, the *Sun* has serious doubts about a railroad being constructed to the Grand Canyon in this generation.[317]

The editor's pessimism about the Williams railroad was manifested again when he ran a bit of sarcasm soon afterwards:

> P. D. Berry is in town from the Grand Canyon this week and will await the building of the Williams & Grand Canyon railroad before he returns.[318]

The editor of the *Gem* joined in the fun, firing the following salvo of sour grapes at Flagstaff's sister city,

> Why don't Williams give excursions over its Grand Canyon railroad?[319]

The joke, ultimately, would be on these Flagstaff die-hards, but there were many hurdles to clear before Williams had the last laugh.

Hardly had the tourist season gotten underway in 1898 when the Spanish-American War broke out, Spain declaring war on April 24. It might seem that this remote conflict, fought in Cuba and the Philippines, would have little to do with faraway Flagstaff, but many Flagstaff men enlisted in the Arizona Rough Riders, including stagecoach driver Howard Marine.[320] It was feared that wartime conditions might have a dampening effect on tourism, although the *Sun* reported hopefully in July:

> Flagstaff, the gateway to the Grand Canyon of the Colorado, is at the present time filled with tourists from all portions of the Union,

and every train from the east or west adds to the list of sightseers, healthseekers and pleasuremakers.[321]

[The use of the phrase "Flagstaff, the gateway to the Grand Canyon" again is notable. In later years, both Flagstaff and Williams were to contend for the right to use the slogan, "Gateway to the Grand Canyon." The first appearance of something close to this usage that we have found was in the *Coconino Sun* in 1892: "The traffic for that point will hereafter go by the way of Flagstaff, which is truly the gateway to the Grand Canyon of the Colorado river."[322] We have above noted other uses of the term].

In spite of the war, several travel writers visited the Grand Canyon in 1898 and published accounts of their experiences. Their articles shed light on the operation of the line at that time.

One of these travelers produced a newspaper article containing interesting observations and good advice:

> To those who are fortunate enough to make the trip, first choose your month. The stage runs from Flagstaff three times a week, beginning April 1 and stopping November 1. June and September are preferable on account of absence of storms. Next, [choose] your wearing apparel; bloomers are necessary for ladies, as skirts make traveling unsafe on the narrow trails; heavy soled shoes, that lace to the knees; a duck waist, cowboy hat and stout gloves. You should place a knapsack on your shoulder in which to carry specimens.
>
> You can [descend] into the Canyon by four trails, the Bright Angel, Berry [Grandview], Hance and Tanner. I chose the Berry, as it is considered the best.[323]

Burton Holmes, a famous and very experienced travel-writer, took the Grand Canyon-Flagstaff Stage Line in 1898 and had much to say. Of significance, the authors have selected the following:

> For barefaced honest badness, all on the surface, commend me to this frank and open town of Flagstaff, Arizona. We first pass three saloons, then a restaurant and a newstand, and a barber-shop, and then another group of drinking-halls. And there are no screen doors to hide the bars, and no attempt is made to persuade the passing visitor that the men who sit behind the numerous green tables, toying with piles of silver dollars, are money-changers or collectors of revenue. Nor are the men who sit in silent circles around the smaller tables, playing solitaire. No, gambling is not winked at by the municipality, it is boldly smiled upon, and flourishes like a green bay-tree upon a score of green baize tables. Even the smoking-room of our hotel [New Bank Hotel] nightly resounds to the click of the ivory chips along with the chink of silver dollars...."[324]
>
> When there are so many passengers that one coach would be overcrowded, a second coach or 'trailer' is attached, transforming our conveyance into a long train that measures forty-eight feet from the tips of the leaders' noses to the tail-board of the trailer. Unhappy are the mortals who become inmates of that trailer; they assiduously collect all the dust, their view is cut off by the forward coach, and they see little else.[325]
>
> [At Thurber's Camp] The ladies are assigned to single tents, of which a score are scattered about. The men...are led into a canvas caravansary big as a circus tent, where canvas cages for each one of us have been provided.[326]
>
> We write our names in the register of this unique hotel, and then pick up and curiously peruse another volume of handwriting, marked, "John Hance's Visitors' Book."[327]

One day spent on the rim satisfies some minds. We are inclined to

Instead of seating passengers on top of the coach, Thurber would at times attach a second coach as a trailer, as seen here

Another view of a tandem coach

Passengers in the rear coach saw more dust than scenery

The big top at Thurber's Camp, summer 1898

On the porch of the dining hall at Thurber's Camp

Empty mine shack Holmes found in 1898

Empty bunkhouse at the Last Chance Mine 1898

tell ourselves that we have seen all that it is possible to see; and many, feeling thus, depart the next morning after their arrival.[328]

In early morning Captain Hance rounds up his stock and brings them saddled to the camp.[329]

The only lady in our little band of adventurers must bow to the strict rules of Captain Hance and don divided skirts, for the old guide will have no ladies in his train who will not ride astride. He keeps a special skirt on hand for those who do not come provided with the proper costume.[330]

Two or three miles from the little camp of tents where we made our headquarters during our visit in early June, 1898, we find a cosy comfortable hotel, a big log-house, erected and presided over by Mr. Peter Berry.[331]

For a hotel proprietor Mr. Berry was altogether too retiring. We were on the point of leaving the cañon in ignorance of the existence of this place, when, quite by accident, we stumbled upon it during an aimless ramble, but, once discovered, the attractions of this Grand View Hotel, and the Grand View Trail, at the head of which this hotel stands, proved so convincing that in August after our return from the Hawaiian Islands, we came a second time to the Grand Canyon, purposely to explore that section of the cañon reached by the Grand View Trail, under the guidance of Mr. Peter Berry.[332]

Many modern writers have stated that the Grandview Hotel was the terminus of the Grand Canyon-Flagstaff Stage Line. Holmes's account, written in 1898, shows, however, that at that late date the line certainly did not go to the Grandview; in fact, the passengers—even a travel expert like Holmes—did not know of its existence. When Holmes made a second trip to the Canyon in August 1898 for the deliberate purpose of staying at the Grandview, he was delighted with his visit and the comforts that Berry provided to guests, including a European chef, saying: "I cannot say enough in praise of our kind host and of the comforts offered by his log hotel."[333]

During his August 1898 visit, Holmes went down the Grandview Trail guided by Berry and spent the night sleeping in the *deserted* [emphasis added] mine shack on Horseshoe Mesa.[334] This evidence and the Cameron letter referred to in the 1897 chapter above, lead us to conclude that the Last Chance Mine was not in operation in 1897 and 1898.

Holmes mentions that a big circus-like tent was used to house the men, and his staff took a photograph showing it. This giant tent found at the scene in 1898 was a first for Thurber's Camp, and suggests that Thurber was trying to respond to the charge that his accommodations at the camp were inadequate by bringing in the "big-top."[335] Still, it was a far cry from the substantial, permanent accommodation that the situation required.

Stella Dysart, a seventeen-year-old, made a trip to the Grand Canyon from Phoenix with her sister and two brothers in a buckboard in 1898, keeping a delightful and information-filled diary. The group was at the Canyon August 7-10. She noted:

We met the United States Mail Stage on its way to Flagstaff, a trip which it makes every second day...[336]

We came to a fork in the road [at the Canyon], one branch leading to Cameron [Grandview] and the other to the Hance trail.[337]

Now the Hance Hotel at this place is not so large or so grand as the Adams or Ford of Phoenix. To be truthful, it is really only a neat little log cabin. Near it are about a dozen clean-looking tents, furnished for rent to tourists. Business is centered in a small cabin in which is post office and store.[338]

[John Hance] is a queer old man, noted for his much talking and is regarded by all tourists as one of the curiosities of the country. He spends part of his time escorting tourists down his trail to the bottom of the Canyon and keeps mules for that express purpose, charging five dollars apiece for the trip.[339]

United States Government

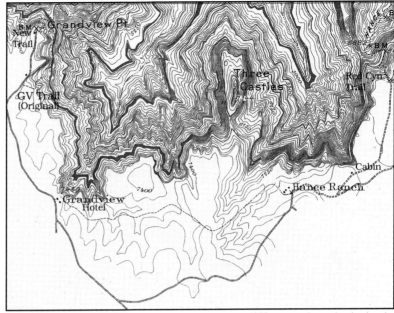

Then [after looking at the Canyon from Lookout Rock] we returned to the wagon and drove to the "camping grounds,' which differ from the other land of the great Coconino Forest only in having pastures fenced in for stock, a pond of water, and four log houses." [This would have been Hull Tank].[340]

A noted writer, T. Mitchell Prudden, traveled to the Grand Canyon in the summer of 1898 and made it clear that the stage did not run to the Grandview, going instead to:

> ...the camp of tents upon the southern brink of the Grand Cañon, where the stage route from Flagstaff ends.[341]

Charles Lummis, who had made the stage journey from Flagstaff to the Canyon in 1892 and 1895, returned in June 1898 with a distinguished party of educators from California, including the president of Stanford University. The party was so impressive that J. W. Thurber himself drove the stage. Lummis wrote:

This map, based on a 1902 survey, shows the landmarks near Thurber's Camp, identified here as Hance Ranch. To the northeast is the new cabin built for Hance when the stage line began using his original cabin. The new cabin was at the head of the Old Hance Trail. The formation shown as "Three Castles" is today called "The Sinking Ship."

> It is a good road, an excellent dinner[342] awaits the traveler at Cedar Ranch; and in the fall of evening the coaches roll down the hill to the piney glade where the Cañon Hotel snuggles in its charming hollow. The hotel is also managed by Mr. Thurber, and the accommodations are surprisingly good.... A hundred yards up an easy slope to the north...we stand on the "rim," looking wistfully down into the shadowy vastness....

> We also went down the Cañon to the river, by the new Hance trail, the best ever constructed in all Arizona. John Hance, the pioneer of this region, is widely known as the ablest and most cheerful prevaricator on the continent, and some of his tales are classic. But he is something more than a picturesque liar—a sincere, earnest and remarkably competent man who has lived alone but unlonely for many years here and has become an inseparable part of the cañon. His trail is a remarkable piece of work; his horses and mules as fine a band as ever did mountain duty, their equipments safe and comfortable, and Hance's own skill the last thing needful.[343]

Land of Sunshine Magazine

A group of young men, this time three friends from Illinois, came in on the train, outfitted themselves in Flagstaff and left for the Grand Canyon on October 22, 1898, following the stage line's road, without a guide. One of them, Sidney Foote, kept a diary. At the Rim, on October 26, they visited Thurber's Camp, which was not open; so they camped there and next morning helped themselves to the New Hance Trail, only to meet John Hance, who was coming up. He charged them $6.50 each to use his trail, then talked at length about how he had worked fifteen years to build it.[344] They found the trail to be difficult and dangerous, one of their burros falling over a ledge, although it

The Lummis party, 1898. This was such an important group of dignitaries that J. W. Thurber himself drove the lead coach. Again one notes the large number of passengers riding on top and imagines their discomfort. Could they take a bath at Thurber's Camp after eating dust all day? The record is silent

The buildings at Thurber's Camp at the close of the 1898 season. The tents are gone and it is reverting to the quiet of its former days. John Hance would soon return to the site and occupy the buildings

Sign tree at the road junction near the Rim, 1898. There are six signs, as follows, from top to bottom:
1—Grand View Hotel 2 mi.
2—Headquarters G C Mining Co.
3—This Road to the Caves
4—Water & Pasture 2 miles
5—Grandview Trail 2 mi.
6—illegible

landed safely a few feet below.

Hostilities in the Spanish-American War ended on August 12, 1898. The nation as a whole had been but lightly affected by the conflict, and it had been good for many businesses. The *Sun*, summing up the local economic situation toward the end of the year, said flatly that, "Flagstaff is experiencing a business boom."[345] But in spite of the short duration of the war, and good business conditions in general, tourism was off. The *Sun* said in November,

> The Grand Canyon stage line has closed for the season. J. W. Thurber, the proprietor, says that the business of the stage line this season has not been profitable, only 267 visitors being carried since the opening in April last.[346]

The editor of the *Citrograph*, a newspaper in Redlands, California, who had been a member of the party of Southern California journalists who took the Grand Canyon-Flagstaff Stage Line in 1895, noticed the above article and ran an editorial about it, concluding,

> We are surprised at the small business done. There is no more wonderful, more picturesque sight on earth than the Grand Canyon of the Colorado. It is a sight never to be forgotten. It is unique. It is unapproachable anywhere on earth for grandeur. We hope next season will see at least a thousand visitors.[347]

To make matters worse, Thurber had dropped his rates from twenty dollars to fifteen for the round trip, according to the 1899 Baedeker's *Guide to the United States*, which quoted 1898 information.

We believe that J. W. Thurber was placed in a critical position at the end of the 1898 season. He knew that he had to upgrade his lodgings for passengers at Thurber's Camp in order to meet the expectations of the traveling public and broaden the appeal of the stage line. He tried to accomplish this with his big tent in 1898, an experiment that apparently failed. He could meet the need for a real hotel by building a big wooden structure, but this would have been a costly proposition, and he was just coming off a season where he had lost money. A ready alternative was at hand, which was that he could take his guests to the nearby Grandview Hotel in 1899. This change would have caused him to sacrifice some revenue he had previously derived from room and board, but it was preferable to undertaking the cost of building a new hotel. Besides, we believe he had a long-term strategy of putting his development eggs into one basket at Bright Angel.

So, the upshot was—as we believe—that Thurber abandoned Thurber's Camp at the end of the 1898 season. The reasons for this abandonment were not stated in any reference material we were able to uncover, but sufficient reasons come readily to mind: First, the stage line had "not been profitable" in 1898, so closing down the camp would have cut costs. Second, Pete Berry had made the Grandview into a hotel that was definitely superior to Thurber's tent camp. Third, Berry had the best and most scenic trail into the Canyon, with the only access to the caves and the mines.

There were other factors that might have had a role in Thurber's decision to close Thurber's Camp at the end of 1898. One was that Thurber had other irons in the fire. He was a major grading contractor, who kept getting sizable jobs. At the end of 1898 he finished a four-year construction project at St. Joseph, moving his outfit back to Flagstaff afterward. The *Sun* said, "He is undecided as to future movements. He may go further west on another contract or disband his men here for the winter. Seventy-one men composed the working force."[348] A company consisting of seventy-one employees, with its animals, equipment, tools, and other gear would have been a very large operation in northern Arizona for the time. Then as now, the trick with a large outfit like this is to keep it working, no small task in a largely undeveloped and sparsely settled region. Once disbanded, Thurber would have found it very difficult to re-gather a force of experienced workers.

Thurber also had personal problems. In December he moved his wife and daughter, Willie, to Los Angeles. The little girl had "dropsy of the heart" and the family doctor advised the Thurbers to take her to a lower elevation for the sake of her health.[349]

As 1898 ended, the railroad project from Williams was still in the news. Though little was happening on the ground, its promoters were full of optimism and they told the world that they had even bigger ideas than they had originally announced. In addition to exploiting their mining properties, they said, they intended to develop the tourism potential of their railroad to Grand Canyon, and would build two hotels there, one at the head of Bright Angel Trail and another at Indian Gardens. They had succeeded in building the smelter at Williams and they confidently predicted that the railroad would be finished by April 1, 1899.[350]

L. H. Tolfree, who had run Camp Thurber until the end of the 1896 season and who had been the proprietor of the New Bank Hotel in Flagstaff since then, was likewise optimistic, saying that he planned to build a two-story annex on the west side of the hotel, adding twenty rooms, bath rooms and other modern amenities. He announced that, "When completed it will be the best equipped hotel between Kansas City and Los Angeles."[351]

The New Bank Hotel in the summer of 1898

1899

Before the 1899 tourist season opened, newspapers carried a story that the Santa Fe Railroad was planning to run a horseless carriage line from Flagstaff to the Grand Canyon and that three large cars and six smaller ones were being built for the purpose.[352] Soon after this, it was reported that the Santa Fe had increased the order to ten cars.[353] If, successful, the auto line would have replaced the horse-drawn stage line. The plan, however, was dropped.

> Los Angeles, May 27—The Santa Fe railway company has abandoned the scheme of operating horseless carriages from Flagstaff to the Grand Canyon. It was announced today that the contractor, who had already started to build the first automobile had given up the contract and so the company concluded to drop the plan for the present.[354]

There is even a possibility that the story was a hoax. Another description of the plan, contained in the *Flagstaff Gem*, reported that Santa Fe officers were going to come to Flagstaff in the summer with the automobiles and make a test run to the Canyon. So far, so good, but then the article went on to something so outrageously impossible that one wonders whether the story was planted by John Hance:

> The horseless carriages will make the descent over Bright Angel's trail, recently described in these columns, and a grand banquet will be given in Indian Gardens, a noted gathering place for travelers and once the home of an extinct race. There is a flavor of romance about the excursion which is highly satisfactory to employees of the railways. Officers are already saving up their dimes for the experience.[355]

However much such stories might have given J. W. Thurber the jitters, automobiles furnished absolutely no competition to his stage line in 1899. The stagecoach was still king and Thurber had the contract for yet another year for the operation of the line tucked in his pocket. Thurber began preparations for the 1899 season in March:

> J. W. Thurber has received eight new buggies, and two seated barouches for his livery business. He informs us that he intends putting on the finest and best equipped line from here to the Grand Canyon this season ever used on this route.[356]

Travelers to the Grand Canyon in this era found this death-defying bridge somewhere along the Rim near Thurber's Camp

50

A tallyho coach. Note the large number of people on top, which was a feature of these big coaches

In addition to the new equipment, he got the relay stations ready, the *Sun* reporting, "J. W. Thurber has his stage line ready for the tourist travel to the Grand Canyon. The stations along the line are being stocked this week."[357] He even sent his own horses and scrapers out to improve the road.[358] He fully expected to have his best season ever, relying in part on the knowledge that the National Teachers' Association's annual meeting in Los Angeles would bring a larger than ever number of Canyon visitors to Flagstaff. The editor of the *Gem* optimistically predicted there would be two or three thousand Grand Canyon tourists during the season.[359] Thurber ordered a local blacksmith, Henry Heller, to build him a large three-decker coach capable of carrying twenty-five passengers, known as a tally-ho, and ordered another one from Los Angeles.[360] These vehicles were intended for local tourism and would be pressed into service on the Grand Canyon run, only in the event all the seating on his other coaches was taken. For local trips, Thurber used the New Bank Hotel as his terminus.[361] We believe that this practice may have given rise to the false belief that the New Bank Hotel was the terminus for the Grand Canyon stage line.

The season got off to a grand start, and Thurber reported that by the end of April he had broken his previous record for the number of tourists taken to the Canyon.[362] For some unknown reason, his manager, George K. Woods, resigned at the first of May, to be replaced by Mr. Miller from Los Angeles.[363] Woods was reported to be working for Thurber again in 1900, so he must have re-entered his employment.

In 1899 the Grand Canyon-Flagstaff Stage Line, for the first time in its history, ran from Flagstaff to the Grandview Hotel rather than to Thurber's Camp.

Five pieces of evidence supporting this belief are:

(1) Thurber ran the following newspaper ad throughout the 1899 tourist season:

> The Grand Canyon and Grand Canyon stage line has in service a line of new six-horse stages. The trip is made in four relays, leaving Flagstaff on Monday, Wednesday and Friday at 7 a.m., returning leaves the rim of the Canyon every Tuesday, Thursday and Saturday, consuming about eleven hours in making the trip. The stop at the rim of the canyon is made at Berry's camp where all guests will be comfortably entertained at the hotel at $3 per day, American plan. Lunch is provided at Cedar Ranch (half way) at 75 cents each.[364] [No doubt it was called a camp because Berry added a number of tents to the log-cabin hotel in order to take care of the overflow. See photos].

(2) The fact that the post office called "Tourist" at Thurber's Camp was closed effective April 12, 1899, just as the tourism season began.[365]

(3) Harriet Monroe's observations in *Atlantic* magazine, giving an account of her May 1899 visit, when she stayed at the Grandview and walked over to the site of Thurber's Camp, which she found to be deserted:

> ...there below me lay the hollow and the cabin. I passed it, the little silent lodge, with rough-hewn seats under the broad eaves of its porch, its doors hospitably unlatched, its rooms still rudely furnished; but all dusty, voiceless, forsaken.[366]

(4) The entries in John Hance's guest book, kept at Thurber's Camp, end at the conclusion of the 1898 season.[367] G. K. Woods, manager of the stage line, brought Hance's book back to Flagstaff and edited it for publication, adding a few essays and illustrations, something he was not likely to have done if Thurber's Camp were still active and the book were still being used. This is the sort of thing one does at the end of an era.

Coach in the forest north of Flagstaff

(5) The following statements by George Wharton James, a man who spent a great deal of time at the Grand Canyon in the 1890s and knew the situation there intimately:

> The Red Canyon Trail...was the trail used in the years 1895-1898 by the tourists who were taken to the Canyon by stage from Flagstaff. [It] was abandoned by the railway officials and their tourists taken to the Grandview Trail.[368]

In addition to these bits of evidence, the persistent statement that the Grand Canyon-Flagstaff Stage Line ran to the Grandview Hotel may be durable and widespread because it had some substance. We believe that the evidence suggests that the Grandview Hotel was the terminus for the stage line only in the years 1899 and 1900, however.

Pete Berry preparing to lead a tourist party down the Grandview Trail

Although Thurber began taking stagecoach passengers to the Grandview Hotel in 1899, he was still operating the Bright Angel Hotel at the site of today's Village. What is not clear is how Thurber would coax tourists coming from Flagstaff on the stage line to stay at the Bright Angel. As it took about two and a half hours to make the fourteen-mile stage trip from Grandview to the Bright Angel, it seems unlikely that passengers would have wanted to tack on that extra time at the end of a wearying journey to the Grandview that had already taken eleven hours. Perhaps a permitted surmise is that they were delivered to the Grandview Hotel and that Thurber made it clear to them that his coach would take them to the Bright Angel during their stay if they wished to see another part of the Canyon or wanted to go into the Inner Canyon on the Bright Angel Trail.

There was talk of building yet another railroad in 1899. With the announcement came an interesting bit of information about one of the pioneer Grand Canyon tour guides, William Hull. It seems that Hull was still acting as a guide to the Canyon, as it was he who took J. L. Woodward of Los Angeles to the Canyon from Williams to check out the proposed railroad route.[369]

Al Doyle, a Flagstaff pioneer who knew the region like the back of his hand from years of travel and exploration, also seemed optimistic about Grand Canyon tourist trade, so much so that in April 1899 he laid out a new wagon road from Flagstaff to the Canyon, which he claimed would cut twelve miles from the trip. The route was described thus,

> The new road leaves the present road a few miles west of the A-1 water troughs and skirts Kendrick mountain, and by the way of Rain Tanks to the Cameron [Grandview] Trail.[370]

The *Sun* reported in April that a consolidation of major existing railroads had occurred and that a new entity had emerged. From now on, the line that would be serving Flagstaff and sponsoring the Grand Canyon-Flagstaff Stage Line was the Santa Fe Pacific Railroad.[371] A couple of weeks after this announcement, J. W. Thurber personally took an official of the new railroad, together with some the magnate's guests, on the stage coach to the Canyon to show him the operation.[372]

Soon after the stage line began rolling in 1899, business was so brisk that Thurber began running stages every day.[373]

L. H. Tolfree, although he had been announcing big plans for the improvement of the New Bank Hotel, quit Flagstaff, leaving town to take over the proprietorship of the Hotel Lindon in Los Gatos, California. He,

The view from East Cedar Ranch, September 1998. The authors can attest that it is a lonely place. You are looking northeast, with Mesa Butte in the back

Another view of East Cedar Ranch during the coaching days

his wife, and daughter Gertrude moved away after a farewell party given them in May.[374] His place at the New Bank Hotel was taken by F. B. Biestman, who had been with the Fred Harvey organization.[375]

The operation of the lunch station at Cedar Ranch, described as a bleak and lonely place by all who visited it, seemed to burn-out the people who manned it. In 1899 the management went again to the Prime family, Mrs. D. R. Prime, and her daughter Alta.[376]

The stage line in 1899 had its by-now usual complement of travel writers. Harriet Monroe, a Chicago poet, wrote an article published in *Atlantic* magazine. Some of her pertinent observations in the article follow:

> We had passed the halfway house [East Cedar Ranch], where, finding the shanty too hot, we had unpacked and eaten our luncheons out in the sun and wind.

> ...our tired horses thrice gave way to fresh ones, and their keepers came out from little shacks to unbuckle the harness and hear the news.

> At last we reach the third relay station [Moqui], and take on six horses instead of four, for the final pull uphill. We alight, and run up and down the shaggy little slope, and free our bodies from the long strain.

> ...the log-cabin hotel welcomed us to our goal. [The Grandview Hotel was the only log-cabin hotel; so this makes it clear that the stage line ran Ms. Monroe and her fellow passengers to the Grandview].

> The benevolent landlady told of a trail which led to Point Lookout, a mile and a half away, beneath whose cliffs the old deserted inn lay in a hollow.[377]

Another travel writer, this one anonymous, described his trip in the summer of 1899, mentioning with admiration the proficiency of his driver, Dixon, about whose skills he said, "...so well does he know his road that he hauls up at the relay stations almost with the exactness of a railroad train on schedule time." The writer and his five fellow passengers were taken to the Grandview Hotel, and it is interesting to note the significant differences surrounding the arrival at the hotel site. All the previous writers who had gone to Thurber's Camp spoke of finding the log cabins and tents down in a bowl and having to walk uphill a hundred yards or so to see the canyon. At the Grandview, the experience was this:

> We passed *down* into a little dell, then up a sylvan slope with grass and belated wild flowers carpeting the ground, and then along a level stretch of road.... [W]e reached the group of tents surrounding a log cabin where we were to put up for the night. The cañon itself was just beyond. We wanted to get a glimpse of it anyhow before darkness set in. It was but a step *below* the enclosure. We hastened down to the edge of the precipice...."[378] [Emphasis added].

On June 1, 1899, an important event occurred that was to have far-reaching consequences for the Grand Canyon-Flagstaff Stage Line: ground was broken for the construction of the Santa Fe & Grand Canyon Railroad from Williams.[379] After months of preparation and talk, workers for the coalition of Lombard, Goode and citizens of Williams began to make the dirt fly. The *Gem* described the situation thus:

> Work was commenced on Tuesday morning on the Santa Fe & Grand Canyon railroad by the contractor, Mr. Richards. A force of eight teams and a number of men were put to work breaking dirt at a point just on the east edge of Williams. Mr. Richards has the contract for the first fifteen miles of the road. The citizens of Williams are very much elated over the prospects for the building of the long-needed road from their town to the Grand Canyon.[380]

Pete Berry, in addition to running the Grandview Hotel, resumed operation of the Last Chance Mine below Grandview Point in 1899.[381] Berry also acted as a guide, taking tourists down the trail to the caves and the mine. In addition to viewing the Canyon scenery, tourists enjoyed the experience of rubbing shoulders with actual Wild West miners, a bonus that no doubt added to the allure of the Grandview as a destination.

By mid-summer, Thurber knew that the doldrums of 1898 had been shaken off. The *Sun* reported:

> For the past two weeks there has been an unprecedented number of visitors to the Grand Canyon of the Colorado river. The average has been thirty tourists a day. The great rush is caused by delegates to the National Convention of teachers to be held at Los Angeles next week. The stage line has been taxed to its utmost capacity and stages from Albuquerque have been added to the line by J. W. Thurber and daily stages are the order of the day. It is expected that the tourists will continue to come during the months of July and August and the travel is away beyond the estimate placed by the railroad company.[382]

A six-horse tandem heading toward Flagstaff

Thurber had his finest year in 1899, conveying almost nine hundred passengers from Flagstaff to the Grand Canyon by the time he shut down operations on October 13.[383] He fell short of the prediction that he would have three or four thousand passengers, but nearly met the mark of one thousand forecast by the *Citrograph* in 1898.

No doubt Thurber was in an optimistic frame of mind at the end of the 1899 tourist season. He could not have failed, however, to notice a little item in the *Sun* that appeared in November. It stated, "The laying of steel on the Williams and Grand Canyon railroad is being pushed. Twelve miles of track has been completed."[384] Work on the new railroad would continue throughout the winter, and those twelve miles of steel would lengthen, and soon spell the doom of the Grand Canyon-Flagstaff Stage Line. Thurber himself aided in the construction of the railroad that would put his stage line out of business, working as a subcontractor on the construction of the Grand Canyon line in the winter of 1899-1900.[385]

Not everyone was sharing in the new prosperity of the tourist business. In Flagstaff, the operator of the New Bank Hotel was suffering. While the venerable hostelry had enjoyed a virtual monopoly of Grand Canyon tourist business in Flagstaff in 1898 and 1899, enjoying boom times, the Flagstaff Hotel [renamed the Commercial Hotel in July 1900] was about to open half a block to the east and the Weatherford Hotel would open on January 1, 1900, a block to the north. Both were bigger and finer than the New Bank Hotel.

The Weatherford Hotel as it appeared for its grand opening, January 1, 1900

1900—The End of the Grand Canyon-Flagstaff Stagecoach Line

As the season of 1900 approached, J. W. Thurber was still running the Grand Canyon-Flagstaff Stage Line. Early in March, as part of the hotel division of his tourism operation, Thurber hired a manager for the kitchen and dining room of the Bright Angel Hotel, Fred Lummitsch, though Thurber himself would manage the hotel.[386] The winter was so mild that a few custom trips were made to the Canyon, even in January, when Lummitsch personally escorted a group there.[387] The regular coach line, with the relay stops and all the accouterments got its earliest start ever, the first guest signing the Bright Angel's register on March 4, 1900.[388]

Thurber made a major change to the Grand Canyon-Flagstaff Stage Line in 1900: in addition to the stage running from Flagstaff to the Grandview, he began running coaches to the Canyon from the End of Track

The Commercial Hotel. It was originally called the Hotel Flagstaff, as shown the sign painted on the east wall

Sherry G. Mangum

Anita (the former Anita's Junction) in the fall of 1998. It is located on a broad flat plain

GCM 2436A

End-of-Track ticket with coupon for stage line

on the Williams-Grand Canyon railroad. He took these End of Track stages at first to the Grandview Hotel as well as the Bright Angel.[389]

The End of Track was first at Anitas Junction [a place now called Anita], some forty-five miles out from Williams, and only about twenty miles from the Bright Angel Hotel.[390] The remaining twenty-mile run to the Bright Angel could be made by a single team of horses, over easy country, with no relays or stops needed in between. From the End of Track to the Grandview Hotel would have meant a journey of about thirty-five miles. It is not clear whether Thurber ran the End of Track stage to the Bright Angel, dropped off passengers who wanted to stay there, then changed horses and took a fresh team for the remaining fourteen miles to Grandview; or whether he used different coaches, teams and routes to service the two hotels, running one branch to the Bright Angel and the other directly from the End of Track to the Grandview.

The new Santa Fe & Grand Canyon Railroad began to run trains from Williams to the End of Track on March 15, 1900,[391] which would also have been the date when Thurber began to run coaches from Anita. Short of rolling stock, the fledgling railroad leased some cars from the Santa Fe Pacific, but was an independent operation. It reached a joint-ticket agreement with the Santa Fe, and starting in May, the Santa Fe ran the following ad every week in a Flagstaff newspaper:

> Excursion rates to the Grand Canyon of Arizona via Williams is given from all points along the Santa Fe railroad. Round trip tickets to the Grand Canyon via Williams from Flagstaff, $12.50 for adults, and children $11.25.[392]

Soon after this, the Flagstaff newspaper carried a little article to the effect that George K. Woods, manager of the Grand Canyon-Flagstaff Stage Line for Thurber, had purchased Thurber's stables in Flagstaff.[393] In July, Thurber rented his home in Flagstaff to another person.[394] In light of what happened later, one wonders whether these events were harbingers of an unannounced decision that Thurber had made to move away from Flagstaff. In September, Thurber was elected as a delegate to the territorial Democrat convention as a resident of Williams.[395]

Even though the railroad was taking people to the end of track from which they could take a short stage jaunt to the Canyon, some travelers were still taking the Flagstaff stage line to the Grandview. The *Sun* gave an example of how that line was being used in July 1900, when it reported that a party of tourists, after having been in Flagstaff for some time,

> ...left for the Grand Canyon today. Like many others, they prefer the trip from this place by stage rather than by rail from Williams.[396]

In Flagstaff, one of the original key players in the Grand Canyon-Flagstaff Stage Line, the New Bank Hotel, was on hard times. It had a narrow escape from the fate that had destroyed the Grand Canyon Hotel: a fire broke out in the cellar under the kitchen and threatened the building. Fortunately for landlord Biestman, the Town of Flagstaff had installed a municipal water system in 1898 and was much better able to fight fires thereafter; the fire fighters quenched the blaze with only a $2,000 loss, most of it to the hotel's stock of liquor, cigars and supplies.[397] Even so, the loss was too much for Biestman, who abandoned the hotel and moved.[398] This opened the door for the re-appearance of L. H. Tolfree, and family, including daughters Gertrude and Edith, who stepped into Biestman's shoes in March, 1900.[399] The Tolfrees stayed at the New Bank Hotel until June, when they gave up the lease and took over the Parker House in Williams, moving the furniture of the New Bank Hotel to the Parker House.[400] J. T. McWilliams was the next player in this game of musical chairs; he leased the New Bank Hotel, and began fitting it for an August 1 reopening date.[401] Soon after this, the *Sun* mentioned that J. T. McWilliams would not reopen the New Bank Hotel as advertised. Instead, he closed it and sold the bar and fixtures to J. J. "Sandy" Donahue to use in the Commercial Hotel.[402] The new hotels, the Commercial and the Weatherford, had driven the New Bank Hotel out of business.

The prospect of an automobile line from Flagstaff to the Grand Canyon surfaced again in 1900, when S. E. Faroat came to town in July from New York and promoted the idea heavily.[403] We give only a passing mention to Faroat here, as we have a separate chapter on auto travel from Flagstaff to the Canyon in this book, to which we refer interested readers.

About the same time Faroat was in town, Flagstaff citizens received word that C. A. Higgins, the assistant general passenger agent of the Santa Fe, the man responsible for much of the early—and very effective—Grand Canyon advertising for the benefit of the railroad and the stage line, had died of typhoid-pneumonia in Chicago at the age of forty.[404]

The builders of the Grand Canyon railroad were still making confident announcements to the world in the spring of 1900, even though they knew that by doing so they were masking an unpleasant reality. In April, the chief engineer appeared in Flagstaff according to the newspaper,

> He says work is progressing finely on the last section of the new road, and that ten miles of the twenty-five of uncompleted grade is ready for track laying, and the road will be completed not later than July 1.[405]

A later article gave a likewise hopeful report about the progress of the railroad:

> J. M. Simpson came in from the Grand Canyon Wednesday. He says that the end of the railroad track is now twelve miles from the canyon, and trains are run to the end of the track, the balance of the trip being made by stage. Just when the railroad will be completed to the canyon is not known, but it will probably be finished some time in July. The tourist traffic over the road is not large at present, but on completion of the road to the canyon a decided increase is expected.[406]

MNA MS 26-29b

The stage leaving the Grandview Hotel

When July came, the news of the railroad was not of progress, but of difficulty. In its issue of July 7, the *Sun* reported it had learned that all construction work on the line was suspended pending the payment of sums due to contractors. The *Gem* noted that

> We are informed that many of the men who have been working on the Grand Canyon railroad have ceased to work on account of not getting their pay, and many are offering to sell their pay checks at twenty cents on the dollar and even for less than this amount. The company seems to be involved to a considerable amount.[407]

The next news about the railroad's troubles was that several liens had been filed against the Tusayan Development Company, L. N. Goode & Co., and the railroad company.[408] Within a week, $120,000 worth of liens had been filed, with more to come.[409] The trouble stemmed primarily from the failure of the vaunted copper mines to live up their revenue projections. The lien filing forced construction to stop at a point on the line called Coconino Siding, 8.63 miles of track beyond Anita, which became frozen as the End of Track,[410] a tantalizing ten miles away from the Canyon, until the legal and financial mess could be untangled. Thurber then began to run his Bright Angel Stage Line from Coconino Siding to his hotel, a very easy two-hour journey.

In July 1900, the newspapers announced that Pete Berry had initiated his own stage service from the End of Track to the Grandview Hotel, buying teams and stages to get it running.[411] It is unlikely that Berry would have done this voluntarily and one can reasonably conclude that he was forced to take this action. We take it to mean that Thurber had quit running passengers from the End of Track to Berry's Grandview Hotel, taking them instead only to his own Bright Angel. After this change, Thurber renamed his End-of-Track coach operation, calling it the Bright Angel Stage Line.[412] The *Sun* tried to help Berry, who was clearly put at a disadvantage by the move, the editor writing,

> Mr. Berry has an excellent hotel, its location being convenient to the only good trail leading down into the Grand Canyon. Tourists and others visiting the canyon should go to the Grand View.[413]

The fact that Pete Berry started running his own stage service from the End of Track to the Grandview Hotel reflected an end of cordial relations between Berry and Thurber. Berry later said that he believed that the cause of the rift was the insistence of the Santa Fe that he be squeezed out, [414] rather than any change of feeling on the part of Thurber.

Al Doyle was hard at work in the summer of 1900 improving his new road from Flagstaff to the Grand Canyon.[415] In those days it was still possible to lay out a roadway across public land wherever one wanted to go, and even to claim the route as a private toll road. There is no record that Doyle obtained any kind of easement or permit for his road. He just scouted it, scratched it out and then improved it. It is not clear what the financial incentive was for Doyle to develop this road. Perhaps he intended to make it a toll road, a practice with which he was familiar, having developed a toll horse trail to the top of the San Francisco Peaks in 1892.[416] It may be that he was working with S. E. Faroat, building a road intended for automobile travel.[417]

The energetic Thurber, never content to have just a few irons in the fire, entered into a contract with the Santa Fe Pacific to grade the tracks for the railroad's new roundhouse in Gallup.[418]

The Santa Fe & Grand Canyon Railroad was forced into receivership on September 5, 1900.[419] The Santa Fe Pacific was the major creditor of the failing line, poised to pick up the pieces.[420] Even though the Santa Fe & Grand Canyon Railroad went into receivership, the receiver kept trains running along the finished track to Coconino Siding. After the legal proceedings began, these trains were those of Santa Fe Pacific rather than the Santa Fe & Grand Canyon Railroad.[421]

The Santa Fe Pacific had been selling combination train-stage tickets to the Grand Canyon since March 15, 1900. Purchasers could buy these tickets at any Santa Fe ticket office. They allowed the buyers to take the main line to Williams, then transfer there to the Grand Canyon railroad and take it to the End of Track, where they would transfer to a stage coach and be taken to the Canyon, to the lodging of their choice, everything being handled in one, simple prepaid transaction. Apparently these combination tickets were good on all of the stages that met the line at the End of Track at first: Berry's to the Grandview, Thurber's to the Bright Angel, and Bass's to Bass Camp. In October 1900, however, the receiver notified Pete Berry in writing that the combination train-stagecoach tickets sold by the receiver-operated railroad were good only for Thurber's Bright Angel Stage Line.[422] It is presumed that a similar letter was sent to Bass. This gave a huge competitive advantage to Thurber. No reasons for this change were given in the letter, but it would seem that the receiver applied this restriction at the behest of the Santa Fe, for everyone familiar with the situation assumed that the Santa Fe would buy the Grand Canyon railroad when the receiver put its assets up for sale to pay its debts. The Santa Fe still had a contract with Thurber to run the stage line and was throwing its weight behind Thurber's operation, with an eye to the future, when the Santa Fe itself would take over all Grand Canyon tourism.

Thurber enjoyed another good season in 1900, the guest register at the Bright Angel Hotel showing that seven hundred and fifty-nine guests signed in.[423] In addition renting rooms and selling meals at the Bright Angel, Thurber operated a lucrative livery stable and guide service at the Canyon, renting mounts, gear and guides to tourists who wanted to go into

Peabody, Glimpses of the Grand Canyon

At the head of the original Grandview Trail

the Canyon via the Bright Angel Trail.[424] He also sold curios, another source of revenue.[425] In addition to this income from his base at Bright Angel, he would have received the ticket money for transporting passengers on the original stagecoach line from Flagstaff to the Grandview.[426] Thurber was sitting pretty.

We believe that at the end of the 1900 season, Thurber shut down the Grand Canyon-Flagstaff Stage Line for good, and that when he did so, he simply walked away from its fixtures, abandoning the structures at Little Spring, East Cedar Ranch and Thurber's Camp.[427] He also seems to have abandoned his rights in the Red Canyon Trail, even though it was still in good repair, as shown by the fact that it was continually in use for mining purposes.[428] From the end of 1900, all of Thurber's operation was at the Bright Angel.

J. W. Thurber seems to have moved his residence from Flagstaff to California at the end of 1900, perhaps for the health of his daughter. The *Sun* mentioned him in a little squib in December 1900 thus, "J. W. Thurber, of Long Beach, Cal., was in town Monday on his way to Albuquerque."[429]

John Hance, the venerable old pioneer Grand Canyon guide, was adapting to all these changes. He still had mining interests, and his asbestos mine was a valuable property, but his guide business must have dropped like a stone when the stage line closed Thurber's Camp at the end of the 1898 season. It seems that Hance helped himself to the abandoned buildings at the camp after Thurber stopped using them, and moved back there from his little cabin at the trailhead, occupying the larger log structure that Thurber had built as a kitchen and dining room.[430] It has been reported that John Hance worked as a trail guide for Pete Berry at the Grandview at times.[431] Perhaps he followed the shift to the Bright Angel. One of the Cameron brothers stated that Hance began to hang around the Bright Angel Hotel about 1900.[432] The *Sun* reported in 1901 that,

> John Hance, the Grand Canyon guide, spent a couple of days here this week. He is busy these days showing tourists the depths of the canyon.[433]

East Cedar Relay Station after abandonment

1901

At the beginning of 1901, the Santa Fe made it official: the Grand Canyon-Flagstaff Stage Line was extinct; all Grand Canyon traffic with which the railroad was connected would be over the rails from Williams. Santa Fe officials inserted the following Announcement, dated January 1, 1901 in the railroad's widely circulated pamphlet *Grand Cañon of the Colorado River, Arizona:*

> The tri-weekly stage line heretofore operated between Flagstaff and the Grand Cañon has been discontinued.
>
> The trip is now made from Williams, Ariz., a town on the main line of the Santa Fe Route, thirty-four miles west of Flagstaff.
>
> Tourists are transported from Williams over the Santa Fe & Grand Cañon R. R. for a distance of fifty-seven miles to the present terminus of that line, and thence by stage to the rim of the Cañon, about ten miles farther.
>
> At present the combined rail and stage ride, Williams to the Cañon, only requires about four and one-half hours time. Trains run daily in each direction, leaving Williams 12:30 p.m. and reach Williams 6:30 p.m.
>
> By this route the Cañon is reached near the head of Bright Angel Trail, a dozen miles west of the former terminus, which affords a very picturesque means of descending from the rim to the river.

Horses, mules, burros and guides may be obtained here.

Comfortable temporary accommodations for visitors have been provided on the rim of the Cañon, pending the construction of improved hotel facilities.

The fare between Williams and the Cañon is at present $10.00 for the round trip; hotel accommodation at the Cañon, $3.00 per day, American plan.

It is proposed to operate an automobile line between Flagstaff and Grand Cañon, of which due announcement will be made later.

Stop-overs are granted on all classes of railroad tickets, also on sleeping-car tickets, at both Williams and Flagstaff, to enable passengers to visit the Cañon. Apply in advance to train and Pullman conductors.

Pullman accommodations for resumption of journey may be reserved through Santa Fe Pacific agents at points named.[434]

The stage line's little office building just west of the depot in Flagstaff was removed from the platform, and the space was left empty.[435] We presume, though we have not found the records to show it, that the stage line's office in the Babbitt Building was also closed.

America, Her Grandeur and Beauty

Thurber's Bright Angel Stage Line coach and team at the Bright Angel Hotel. The harness on the lead horse has the initials G.C.S.L. stamped on it, for the "Grand Canyon Stage Line."

Although the stage line from Flagstaff had ceased operations, Thurber was in an enviable position as 1901 dawned. He had the exclusive stage line for which the Grand Canyon railroad honored combination rail-stage tickets to the Canyon. He had a destination hotel only ten miles from the End of Track. And he received the huge majority of the Grand Canyon tourists at the Bright Angel Hotel, where in addition to providing room and board to them, he could generate additional income by selling souvenirs, renting horses and outfits, and providing guided tours.

Thurber began his preparations for the 1901 tourist season in mid-March by sending George K. Woods, who had previously been the manager of the Grand Canyon-Flagstaff Stage Line, to the Bright Angel Hotel to act as the manager of the Bright Angel Stage Line.[436] The stage coach operation, though extremely important to both the railroad and the hotel, was now greatly simplified, with a minimum of animals, men and equipment needed to make the short run from the end of track to the Bright Angel.

In addition to his tourist business, Thurber's contracting enterprise was flourishing, and he landed a major contract with the Santa Fe Pacific Railroad to construct a new grade for the "Peavine" Railroad to Prescott. This project encompassed many miles of railbed, as the Santa Fe bypassed the old Rock Butte route on the new path over the Hell's Canyon bridge.[437] Thurber had one hundred teams of horses at work on the big job.[438]

Pete Berry, gearing up for the 1901 season at the Grandview Hotel, got his friends at the *Sun* to announce at the end of March that he was open for business and would again furnish free stage service from the end of track direct to "the best hotel on the rim of the canyon."[439]

Some time between March 23 and April 13, 1901, in spite of his near-monopoly of the new Canyon tourism, J. W. Thurber decided to sell a half interest in his Grand Canyon enterprises. The *Sun* made the announcement of the event on the latter date:

George K. Woods and wife, returned from Bright Angel hotel, Grand Canyon, where Mr. Woods has been manager of the

GCM 8606

The Bright Angel Stage in the forest

Thurber stage line. J. W. Thurber this week sold a half interest in his stage line and hotel to Martin Buggeln, of Williams, and he has taken charge of the business at the Canyon.[440]

No reasons for Thurber's selling were mentioned by the newspaper, and we have seen none in any other place. Maybe, due to his long experience of dealing with the Santa Fe Pacific, he foresaw trouble ahead in working with the company. Maybe he had had his fill of the tourist business. Maybe he wanted to concentrate on his construction business. Maybe he had to move to California for his daughter's health. Maybe Buggeln made him such an attractive offer that he felt that he could not refuse it.

A couple of months later, in June, with the tourist season of 1901 in full swing, the other shoe dropped, with Thurber selling the remaining half of his Grand Canyon interests to Buggeln, the *Sun* reporting,

> J. W. Thurber spent Tuesday here. He has sold his interest in the Grand Canyon stage line and hotel at Bright Angel to Martin Buggeln. Mr. Thurber now has his headquarters at Ash Fork, and is well along with the contract of grading the cut-off on the Santa Fe, Prescott & Phoenix Railroad. Mrs. Thurber and children, who are living at Long Beach, California, will spend the next two months camping out at various points on the rim of the Grand Canyon.[441]

Thurber's sale of the remaining half of his business cut all his ties with the Grand Canyon. Apparently he severed his connections with the town of Flagstaff as well. In those days, the *Sun*, like many small-town newspapers, was rather starved for local news. As a result, the editor would drop into the hotels periodically to look at the guest registers and write a blurb about who was in town. Such an article appeared in May 1901, showing that Thurber had registered at the Commercial Hotel, listing his address as Long Beach, California.[442] In time, Thurber would migrate completely to California, moving his business and his residence there.[443]

The party of artists at the Grand Canyon, at the Grandview Hotel. John Hance stands to the left. The man with the beard behind the burro is Thomas Moran, seated is Inness, to the right is M'Cord

James Wilbur Thurber reigned as the principal figure in the history of the Grand Canyon-Flagstaff Stage Line from 1895 to its end in 1900; brought its successor, the Bright Angel Stage Line, into existence; and pioneered the development of tourist facilities at Grand Canyon Village. Although he is not nearly so well known as some of the other Grand Canyon pioneers, such as Ralph Cameron, John Hance and Pete Berry, we think he was a very significant individual in the history of Grand Canyon tourism and deserves more recognition than historians have so far accorded him.

The Santa Fe had been promoting its combination railroad-stage coach tickets to the Grand Canyon since 1892, the arrangement whereby passengers would take the train to Flagstaff, then transfer to the stage for the Canyon. In 1901, its advertising mill switched seamlessly to the promotion of the new rail-stage service from Williams. In May, it sponsored a trip to the Canyon by noted artists Thomas Moran, G. M. M'Cord, and George Inness, Jr., together with an editor of *Century* magazine. The purpose was a bold one, as announced by one of the artists:

> "We expect to complete a piece of work this time," said Mr. Inness, "which will surpass in grandeur and scenic effect any reproduction of the Grand Canyon ever attempted. It is a very difficult undertaking, but we have every facility for doing the work and as this is the most favorable season of the year for getting a

good view of the canyon we feel reasonably well assured of success."[444]

Moran, while he was in Flagstaff, dropped in on the editor of the Sun and discussed the trip with him, revealing that this would be his last journey to his beloved Grand Canyon. The editor surmised that age was forcing Moran to make the unhappy decision.[445] (It was not Moran's last trip).

The railroad's advertising efforts were successful, for the tourist business at Grand Canyon in the summer of 1901 was good. The bounty even spilled over to the disadvantaged Pete Berry, who visited Flagstaff in July and told the editor of the Sun that he had a number of guests at the Grandview and was expecting more.[446]

The fallout from the failure of the Santa Fe & Grand Canyon Railroad continued long into 1901. In January the smelter at Williams was sold at a Sheriff's sale to parties from Yavapai County who stated that they were going to relocate it.[447] Soon afterwards, the loose assets, steel rails, spikes, etc., were sold at another Sheriff's sale.[448] In April, Judge Sloan made a key decision in a big lawsuit involving the creditors of the line, determining the priority of claims.[449] With this decision out of the way, the parties knew where they stood in the legal pecking order, and the lawyers then busied themselves negotiating settlements. The next step was to put the major assets of the railroad up for auction, and in June, a legal notice of the impending sale began running in the Sun, letting the world know that 63.25 miles of main line and 2.5 miles of branch to the Anita mine, and six miles of grade would be sold for cash, with a minimum bid of $150,000 required.[450] The sale was held on July 18, and there was only one bidder, E. D. Kenna, an agent for the Santa Fe Pacific and certain major bondholders. These creditors formed a committee which turned their newly acquired assets over to the Santa Fe Pacific for management.[451]

The Santa Fe Pacific then created a new subsidiary corporation called the Grand Canyon Railway, incorporated August 10, 1901, to run the railroad.[452] The Santa Fe Pacific at the time was undergoing its own metamorphosis into the Atchison, Topeka and Santa Fe Railway,[453] although for convenience it was still most often called the Santa Fe.

Although the sale of the railroad to the Santa Fe passed the line from weak into strong hands, it was a bitter pill for the investors in the defunct Santa Fe & Grand Canyon Railroad, most of whom received only pennies on the dollar as a return on their investments. Many of the contractors had to settle for drastic reductions of their claims as well. Hardest hit were several individual citizens of Williams, who had supported the line as a matter of civic betterment and patriotic duty, and not as a sheer investment.[454] For all those who participated in the original construction of the line, it was a disaster.

The people of Williams were dealt an additional hard blow on July 2, 1901, when a fire rampaged through the business district, burning forty-three buildings, virtually the entire downtown. The only substantial building left unharmed was the Grand Canyon hotel.[455] Among the victims was L. H. Tolfree, who was then operating the Tolfree Hotel, and lost everything.[456]

As soon as it became obvious to the world that the Santa Fe was going to take over the railroad to the Grand Canyon, the knowledge stimulated both tourism and mining activity. Before then, outsiders were skeptical of the ability of the promoters to build and run a reliable railroad, but they had no such doubts about the Santa Fe. A properly run railroad would reduce the costs of freighting Grand Canyon ore to processing plants; so investors took another look at the Canyon mines. In June, the twelve asbestos claims of John Hance, C. H. McClure, and the W. H. Ashurst estate, were bonded to Susan W. Selfridge of New York for $6,000.[457] Selfridge followed through by making an outright purchase of the claims in October, for $6,250.[458] John Hance was hired as the manager for the mine, which probably ended or at least sharply curtailed his guiding activities for the duration of his

MNA MS 196-74-1987

John Hance. This is a rare photo, as he usually posed in the saddle or standing ramrod stiff

employment.[459]

Another mining property sale occurred on August 21, 1901, when the Grandview holdings, including the mines, trail, mill sites, and the Grandview Hotel, were purchased by Henry Barbour for $35,000.[460] Indicating how loosely ownership interests in such mining properties were reckoned by the participants, the newspaper said that the owners of the Grandview were R. H. Cameron, Ed I. Gale, P. D. Berry and Niles Cameron.[461] Yet, when the owners ran a legal notice of the sale, the name of Annie M. Cameron [mother of Ralph and Niles] was added to the list.[462] Barbour soon re-sold at a profit to a group headed by John H. Page, who incorporated the Canyon Copper Company and took over the operation of the facilities in 1902.[463] Apparently the terms of the transaction allowed the Berry group to continue to operate the property through the end of 1901.[464]

Pete Berry made another sale in 1901, when he conveyed his interest in the Bright Angel Trail to Ralph Cameron.[465] The details of this transaction are not known, but it was apparently some kind of settling of affairs between the two men, who were still on friendly terms. Cameron would continue to operate the Bright Angel Trail as a toll road and run a hotel at the trailhead. Berry stayed in the Grandview area, homesteaded 160 acres adjacent to the Grandview Hotel and built a small hotel he called The Summit in competition with the Grandview.

The Santa Fe, operating the newly-formed Grand Canyon Railway, wasted no time repairing, upgrading and reconstructing the line from Williams. Much of the construction that had been performed by the failed Santa Fe & Grand Canyon Railroad was substandard and unsuitable for heavy use; so the Grand Canyon Railway first devoted its energies to bringing the existing track up to first-class condition.[466] After this reconstruction was finished, the Grand Canyon Railway crews began building new track, bringing the rails ever closer to the Canyon. The effort succeeded at last, and the long-held dream of a railroad to the Grand Canyon was turned into a reality when the first train making the complete run from Williams steamed into the Grand Canyon station on September 17, 1901.[467]

The end of the stagecoach era at the Grand Canyon: the first train to run all the way from Williams to the Canyon, September 17, 1901

After September 17, 1901, the train dropped all its passengers at the door of the Bright Angel Hotel. There was no longer any reason for Buggeln to run the Bright Angel Stage Line, successor to the Grand Canyon-Flagstaff Stage Line; so he stopped operating it. Pete Berry continued to conduct his own free stage. Instead of running from the End of Track, it now went directly from the Bright Angel to the Grandview Hotel, leaving every morning at 8:30.[468]

The Santa Fe was quick to exploit its new train service to the Canyon, and began scheduling through coaches from Los Angeles:

> The Santa Fe has established a weekly [railroad] car service between Los Angeles and the Grand Canyon of Arizona, to be operated throughout the tourist season. The first through car will leave Los Angeles for the canyon December 3. It is the company's intention to make that city the center for the traffic to and from this point.[469]

The train not only made it easier, faster and cheaper for people to visit the Canyon, but it extended the season as well. Keeping the tracks open, aided by locomotive-propelled snowplows, was feasible. Grand Canyon tourism henceforth would be a year-around affair. The *Sun* passed on to its readers this item in November 1901, giving an indication of the new bounty brought about by the train:

> Martin Buggeln of the Bright Angel Hotel, Grand Canyon, was in town yesterday. There are a large number of visitors at the Grand Canyon at present, and during the winter the number is expected to increase. Three hundred and sixty visitors spent Sunday last at the canyon.[470]

The fall of 1901 saw another new arrival at the Grand Canyon, telephone service from Flagstaff. W. H. Timerhoff, a druggist, had a public phone in his drug store and advertised that people could come to his store and for a small fee call folks at the South Rim.[471]

Just over the horizon was the arrival of the automobile, which would provide yet another cheap, speedy and comfortable way to reach the Grand Canyon. In December 1901, Oliver Lippincott announced that he was preparing an expedition which would make a test run from Flagstaff to Grandview to demonstrate the feasibility of an auto road. He confidently predicted that the trip would be made in three or four hours.[472] If the test run were successful, he said, it would launch a full-fledged auto stage service to the Canyon.[473]

At the end of 1901, those people connected with Grand Canyon tourism could look back and see clearly that it had been a pivotal year, marking the end of an era and the advent of a new age. The day of the horse-drawn vehicle, which had been the accepted mode of travel for a thousand years, was coming to an end everywhere, even in the remote regions of the West.[474] In the first year of the Twentieth Century the Grand Canyon was transformed from a remote, hard-to-reach location into a mainstream tourist attraction available to all.

GCM 15523

Coach with passengers in front of the El Tovar Hotel

Aftermath

The Santa Fe brought the Fred Harvey Company to the Grand Canyon to take care of the tourists it delivered there. In order to handle the huge surge of tourism caused by the completion of the railroad, the Santa Fe bought the Bright Angel Hotel and built the El Tovar, turning the management of both over to Harvey.

Harvey officials purchased a few of the better coaches that had been used on the Grand Canyon-Flagstaff Stage Line and used them to take guests on scenic drives along the Rim, a practice that lasted into the 1920s, when the grand old coaches were phased out and replaced by motor busses. The last stagecoach, relic of the Grand Canyon-Flagstaff Stage Line, rolled to a final stop in 1923.[475]

GCM

One of the last coaches at the Canyon, taking tourists out along the West Rim Drive

Endnotes

1. The authors recommend the following books to readers who are interested in the history of Flagstaff: Ashworth, Donna. *Biography of a Small Mountain.* Small Mountain Books. Flagstaff. 1991; Cline, Platt. *They Came to the Mountain.* Northland Press. Flagstaff. 1976; and *Mountain Town.* Northland Press. Flagstaff. 1994; Mangum, Richard and Sherry. *Flagstaff Historic Walk.* Hexagon Press. Flagstaff. 1993; and *Flagstaff Album.* Hexagon Press. Flagstaff. 1993.

2. General Land Office Map, 1880.

3. Woods, G. K. *Personal Impressions of the Grand Canyon of the Colorado.* The Whitaker and Ray Company. San Francisco. 1899. p. 37.

4. Verkamp, Margaret M. *History of Grand Canyon National Park.* Grand Canyon Pioneers Society. Flagstaff. 1993. p. 11.

5. Verkamp. *op. cit.* p. 11.

6. *Coconino Weekly Sun*, June 9, 1892.

7. The first survey of the Grand Canyon area was made in 1902. *Coconino Weekly Sun,* October 25, 1902.

8. Cleeland, Teri. "To Hull and Back" article in *People and Places of the Old Kaibab.* USDA Forest Service Southwest Region, Report #10. September 1990. p.43. There is a conflict of opinion about the date of this first visit by Ayer. Shock quotes Ayer in Ayer's own autobiography, as stating that the date was 1883: Shock, Donald Paul. *The History of Flagstaff.* Thesis, Northern Arizona University. 1952. p. 133-134. McClintock, who interviewed Ayer, claimed that Ayer remembered the visit as occurring in 1884. We believe the correct date to be 1884, as this is borne out by other evidence, such as the date of Hance's homestead filing.

9. Cleeland. *op. cit.* p. 43.

10. Verkamp *op. cit.* p. 11. Also *Arizona Champion*, January 22, 1887.

11. *Arizona Champion*, May 3, 1884.

12. *Arizona Champion*, June 7, 1884.

13. *Arizona Champion*, June 14, 1884.

14. *Arizona Champion,* December 6, 1884.

15. Woods. *op. cit.* p. 37.

16. Way, Thomas E. *Destination Grand Canyon.* Golden West Publishers. Phoenix. 1990. p. 25.

17. *Coconino Sun*, May 14, 1937.

18. Olberding, Susan Deaver. *A History of Fort Valley, Arizona, and Its Forest Experiment Station 1850 to 1992.* Master's Thesis. Northern Arizona University. 1993. p. 18: "By 1885, a privately-owned tourist stage business operated between Flagstaff and the Grand Canyon Grandview Point overlook passing through the valley via Fort Moroni and using Leroux Springs, possibly on the Beale route.... After leaving Big Leroux Springs, the road climbed a steep hill on its way toward Hart Prairie, and tourists probably walked alongside or helped push the stage up the incline. This route, described as the 'flying stage', continued northwest through Hart Prairie and Cedar Ranch."

19. This is a very small newspaper clipping found in the NAU Special Collections Library, Manuscript File #119, Frier Collection, Box 1, Scrap Book I, page 13.

20. Way. *op. cit.* p. 27.

21. *Arizona Champion*, February 7, 1885.

22. *Arizona Champion*, February 21, 1885.

23. *Arizona Champion*, May 16, 1885.

24. Cameron, Bert, Interview. June 21, 1939. Grand Canyon Park Service Library. Moran, Thomas. *Home Thoughts from Afar, Letters of Thomas Moran to Mary Nimmo Moran.* East Hampton Free Library. East Hampton, NY. 1967. In a letter dated June 5, 1892, Thomas Moran described hiking past these waterfalls, "The trail was easy enough until we struck the first waterfall in the lava. Here we let ourselves down with ropes and in the same way of six waterfalls."

25. *Arizona Champion*, November 14, 1885.

26. *Arizona Champion*, November 21, 1885.

27. *Arizona Champion*, January 23, 1886.

28. *Arizona Champion*, July 17, 1886. The Pullman Company made the famous Pullman car for railroads.

29. *Arizona Champion*, September 11, 1886.

30. *Arizona and the West.* Spring 1978 pp. 41-64 and Summer 1978 pp. 155-172. "Ralph H. Cameron and the Grand Canyon." Douglas H. Strong. p. 42.

31. Tinker, George H. *Northern Arizona in 1887.* Arthur H. Clark Company, Glendale, CA. 1969. pp. 8-9.

32. Verkamp. *op. cit.* pp. 12-13.

33. Greever, William S. *Arid Domain.* Stanford University Press. 1954.

34. Kinsey, Joni Louise. *The Majesty of the Grand Canyon, 150 Years in Art.* First Glance Books. Cobb, California. 1998. p. 28.

35. *Arizona Champion,* November 10, 1888.

36. Woods. *op. cit.* p.64.

37. Records of Yavapai County Transferred to Coconino County, page 187, also page 470.

38. Cleeland. *op. cit.* p. 43.

39. *Arizona Champion*, August 24, 1889.

40. *Arizona Champion*, August 10, 1889.

41. *Arizona Champion,* July 20, 1889.

42. *Arizona Champion*, September 7, 1889.

43. *Arizona Champion*, March 29, 1890.

44. *Arizona and the West.* Spring 1978 pp. 41-64 and Summer 1978 pp. 155-172. "Ralph H. Cameron and the Grand Canyon." Douglas H. Strong. p. 43.

45. Berry File. GCM #58597

46. *Coconino Weekly Sun,* June 20, 1891.

47. *Coconino Weekly Sun,* August 1, 1891.

48. *Coconino Weekly Sun,* June 20, 1891.

49. Schullery, Paul, editor. *The Grand Canyon, Early Impressions.* Colorado Associated University Press. 1981. This book contains the passage concerning the Grand Canyon trip from *Our Italy.* p. 37.

50. *Ibid.* p. 37.

51. *Ibid.* p. 37.

52. *Ibid.* p. 37.

53. *Ibid.* p. 38.

54. *Ibid.* p. 38. Pete Berry, in one of his fragmentary pocket diaries, described a trip he made in a heavily loaded wagon, following a similar route, in May 1892: "24—Left Flagstaff 10 a.m. Camped at Deadman Flat. 25—Came to Red Horse. 26—Got to

the Rim at Hances at 11 a.m."

55. *Ibid.* p. 41.

56. Colton, Harold S. and Baxter, Frank C. *Days on the Painted Desert and In The San Francisco Mountains.* Coyote Range. Flagstaff. 1927. p. 62.

57. Steele, J. W. *Guide to the Pacific Coast.* Rand, McNally & Co. New York. 1891. pp. 118-119.

58. *Coconino Weekly Sun,* November 26, 1891.

59. *Coconino Weekly Sun,* December 17, 1891. The paper erroneously reported that the trail was four miles *west* of Hance's Trail, but the reference must have been to the Red Canyon Trail, which is *east* of Hance's. *See* Records of Coconino County, Book 3 of Deeds page 46, where Hance sold his trail rights to Thurber, Tolfree, and Wheeler. In addition to the Hance Trail, the sale included a one-quarter interest in the Red Canyon Trail.

60. Several reports of prospecting and tourist parties going from Flagstaff to the Canyon are found in the newspapers of the time. See *Coconino Weekly Sun,* January 7; January 14; February 11; March 3; March 10; March 31; April 14; April 28, 1892.

61. As already mentioned, W. W. Bass began running a stage from Williams to Bass Camp in 1892. The Peach Spring stage line was the earliest of all, running from the railroad stop at Peach Spring to Diamond Creek. Its operator was Julius Farlee. Way. op. cit. p. 25. Bass sold his stage service to Sanford Rowe in 1892 and Rowe then took passengers to Rowe Well, some five miles west of today's Village. Anderson. *op. cit.* p. 80. In 1894 Bass moved his base of operations from Williams to Ash Fork. Way. *op. cit.* p. 32.

62. *Scientific American.* June 18, 1892 and August 6, 1892. "The Grand Canyon of the Colorado." Horace C. Hovey.

63. "Aubrey": this old-fashioned term has been replaced. The Aubrey designation was applied to a thick layer of whitish to tan-colored stone, which was then thought to be a single formation. Modern geologists have found that there are distinct layers within what was called the Aubrey, principally Coconino sandstone and Kaibab limestone. *Interview* with Wayne Ranney, geologist.

64. *Coconino Weekly Sun,* January 14, 1892.

65. *Coconino Weekly Sun,* March 17, 1892.

66. *Journal of Arizona History.* Vol. 17, No. 1, Spring, 1976. "Railroad at the Rim, The Origin and Growth of Grand Canyon Village." Gordon Chappell. p. 91.

67. *Coconino Weekly Sun,* March 24; March 31; and April 28, 1892.

68. *Coconino Weekly Sun,* April 14, 1892.

69. *Ibid.*

70. *Coconino Weekly Sun,* May 5, 1892.

71. *Coconino Weekly Sun,* May 5, 1892. The corporation was called the Grand Canyon Hotel Company. The officers of the company were Dr. D. J. Brannen, president; J. H. Hoskins Jr., treasurer; H D. Ross, secretary; Geo. Babbitt, T. A. Riordan, and P. J. Brannen, directors. *Coconino Weekly Sun,* May 12, 1892.

72. *Coconino Weekly Sun,* May 12, 1892.

73. *Coconino Weekly Sun,* May 12, 1892.

74. Schullery. *op. cit.* pp. 37-38.

75. John Hance was in Flagstaff the week that the Grand Canyon-Flagstaff Stage Line was being organized, and it is likely that the Board of Trade's directors negotiated an agreement with him. *Coconino Weekly Sun,* May 5, 1892.

76. *Coconino Weekly Sun,* May 12, 1892. There is no account of Foster working for the stage line after the 1892 season. The *Sun* reported in 1894 that he died of blood poisoning: *Coconino Weekly Sun,* June 28, 1894.

77. *Coconino Weekly Sun,* May 12, 1892.

78. *Ibid.*

79. *Coconino Weekly Sun,* May 19, 1892.

80. *Coconino Weekly Sun,* May 12, 1892.

81. *Coconino Weekly Sun,* May 12, 1892. Higgins, *Personal Impressions of the Grand Cañon of the Colorado.* p. 44. When the group signed the Hance's guest book at the Canyon, they noted "All of Alameda, Cal."

82. *Coconino Weekly Sun,* May 26, 1892.

83. *Coconino Weekly Sun,* June 9, 1892. [Bissell's Point—later known as Zuni Point—was in the old days a favorite place for viewing the Canyon. Hance hacked out a road to it and regularly took visitors there, who waxed rhapsodic about the views from the place. Today the paved East Rim Road bypasses Zuni Point and although it is still shown on the Cape Royal USGS 7.5 topo map, no access to Zuni Point is now provided. The other names given to Canyon features by the Bissell party did not stick and are not found on modern maps. A pattern of naming points after Indian tribes was adopted later, and many of the old names were replaced to conform to it. Thus Rowe's Point became Hopi Point, Sentinel Point became Maricopa Point, and Cremation Point became Shoshone Point].

84. *Coconino Weekly Sun,* May 26, 1892.

85. *Coconino Weekly Sun,* June 2, 1892 and June 9, 1892.

86. *Coconino Weekly Sun,* May 26, 1892.

87. *Coconino Weekly Sun,* June 9, 1892.

88. We believe that the company used Hance's log cabin as an office and storeroom, relocating Hance to a new cabin at his trail-head about half a mile away. The article written in 1893 by Henry Finck, [see 1893 chapter] reported Hance living in a cabin "on the brink." Hance's original cabin was not on the brink but down in a hollow. Whether the hotel company built the cabin for Hance or whether the old guide built it himself, we were unable to learn. We find it credible that the stage company built the new cabin for Hance so that it could use his original cabin as an office and store-room and Hance could be nearby but could have some privacy. During the winter Hance moved into the Inner Canyon, spending his time prospecting and looking after his mining claims.

89. *Coconino Weekly Sun,* May 26, 1892.

90. Woods, G. K. *Personal Impressions of the Grand Canyon of the Colorado.* The Whitaker and Ray Company. San Francisco. 1899. p. 45.

91. *Ibid.* p. 45.

92. D'Emilio, Sandra and Campbell, Suzan. *The Art & Artists of the Santa Fe Railway.* Peregrine Smith Books. Salt Lake City. 1991. p. 8.

93. Weigle, Marta and Babcock, Barbara A. *The Great Southwest of the Fred Harvey Company and the Santa Fe Railway.* The Heard Museum. Phoenix. 1996. p. 7.

94. Farquhar, Francis P. *Books of the Colorado River & the Grand Canyon.* W. M. Morrison Books. Austin, Texas. 1991. p. 23. "In 1892 the Santa Fe Railroad began to play up the Grand Canyon as a tourist attraction. Stage service was established between Flagstaff and the Canyon and primitive accommodations were provided at Hance's Camp near Grand View. Writers and artists were encouraged to take the trip and 'publicity' began to appear. On the permanent staff of the railroad company was C. A. Higgins, who, until his death in 1900, was in charge of advertising. He produced a succession of pamphlets."

95. Lummis, Charles F. *Some Strange Corners of Our Country.* University of Arizona Press. Tucson. 1989. Reprint of 1892 book. p. 18.

96. *Coconino Weekly Sun,* June 23, 1892.

97. *Coconino Weekly Sun,* July 14, 1892.

98. *Coconino Weekly Sun,* September 1, 1892.

99. Hovey. *op. cit.* August 6, 1892. p. 87.

100. *Coconino Weekly Sun,* June 16, 1892.

101. GCM. Pete Berry File #58597

102. *Coconino Weekly Sun,* August 11, 1892.

103. *Coconino Weekly Sun,* July 28, 1892. The story was completed by Harriet Monroe in 1899. She took the Grand Canyon-Flagstaff Stage Line and the driver, "...told the story of a young English preacher whom he once picked up near the end of the road; who, too poor to pay stage fares, was walking to the cañon; who after two days and nights in the thirsty wastes, his canteen empty and only a few biscuits left in his pouch, was trudging bravely on, with blistered feet and aching body, because he 'must see' the mighty miracle beyond." *Atlantic Monthly,* December 1899, p. 816. An even more remarkable story of going from the Grand Canyon to Flagstaff on foot appeared in the *Sun* on August 2, 1894: "T. C. Donahue had a cat which ate his little chickens. He concluded to send the feline to the Grand Canyon, and accordingly the cat was boxed up and sent to nature's wonderland. But somehow Thomas did not like his new home, and in a day or two disappeared, and ten days afterwards he was back at his old home in Flagstaff, feasting on young chickens."

104. *Coconino Weekly Sun,* November 10, 1892.

105. *Coconino Weekly Sun,* November 10 and 17, 1892.

106. *Coconino Weekly Sun,* November 10, 1892.

107. Woods. *op. cit.* p. 63.

108. Woods. *op. cit.* p. 64.

109. Woods. *op. cit.* pp. 44-64. It is hard to tell the exact number, since some guests signed the book with vague statements, such as "John Doe and party." Burton Holmes, who was a guest at Hance's in 1898, pointed out that there were two books at the tourist camp: one the regular hotel register and the other Hance's guest book in which travelers were invited to write their impressions, comments, etc. Holmes, *Travelogue,* p. 137.

110. Woods. *op. cit.* pp. 31-43.

111. Woods. *op. cit.* p. 64.

112. *Coconino Weekly Sun,* July 13, 1893.

113. *Coconino Weekly Sun,* July 13, 1893.

114. *Baedeker's The United States.* Scribner's. New York. 1893.

115. Hall, Sharlot. *Sharlot Herself, Selected Writings.* Sharlot Hall Museum Press. Prescott, AZ. 1992. p. 11.

116. Hall. *op. cit.* pp. 17-18. It should be noted that the years 1891, 1892 and 1893 were years of drought in northern Arizona.

117. Hall. *op. cit.* p. 18. All of the tourists were fascinated by the troughs at East Cedar Ranch, a series of stair-stepped hollow logs going down the slope. See photo. One tourist counted them, and found that there were twenty-four. Her reference to the abandonment of the "old road" to the Cañon may refer to the route via Red Horse.

118. Hall. *op. cit.* pp. 18-19.

119. Hochderffer, George. *Flagstaff Whoa.* Museum of Northern Arizona. Flagstaff. 1965. p. 124.

120. Hochderffer. *op. cit.* p. 124. We think Hochderffer was confused. Lockett's Tanks, which still exist today, are about seven miles south of Moqui.

121. Hochderffer. *op. cit.* p. 125.

122. *Nation.* September 7 and 14, 1893. "From Flagstaff to the Grand Cañon."

123. *Ibid.* p. 170.

124. *Ibid.* p. 170.

125. *Ibid.* p. 187.

126. *Ibid.* p. 188. Did Hance really have 58 mines, or was this one of his famous exaggerations?

127. *Ibid.* p. 188.

128. *Coconino Weekly Sun,* August 24, 1893.

129. *Coconino Weekly Sun,* January 11, 1894.

130. *Coconino Weekly Sun,* August 24, 1893.

131. Chrisman left Flagstaff after the fire. He appeared in Flagstaff again in 1900 and called on his old friends, telling them that he was living in Naco, Arizona, where he was the first settler. *Coconino Sun,* March 3, 1900. In 1901 he came through town, telling old friends that he had spent the previous six months living in Porto Rico. *Coconino Sun,* January 5, 1901.

132. Richard K. Mangum. *Mountain Living Magazine.* "A Hell of a Way to Run A Railroad." Parts One and Two. February and March, 1998.

133. *Coconino Weekly Sun,* October 26, 1893.

134. *Coconino Weekly Sun,* October 12, 1893.

135. *Coconino Weekly Sun,* November 2, 1893.

136. *Coconino Weekly Sun,* November 2, 1892.

137. *Coconino Weekly Sun,* December 7, 1893.

138. *Coconino Weekly Sun,* March 15, 1894.

139. *Coconino Weekly Sun,* March 29, 1894.

140. Coconino Weekly Sun, April 26, 1894.

141. *Coconino Weekly Sun,* April 26, 1894.

142. *Coconino Weekly Sun,* June 7, 1894. Thurber was also running a logging camp, where he was the victim of an accident which broke his jaw in three places and knocked out all his teeth. *Coconino Weekly Sun,* April 19, 1894. To make matters worse, while healing the fracture, he caught the mumps. *Coconino Weekly Sun,* May 17, 1894.

143. *Coconino Weekly Sun,* August 9, 1894.

144. *Coconino Weekly Sun,* June 7, 1894.

145. Coconino Weekly Sun, May 17, 1894.

146. *Coconino Weekly Sun,* May 24, 1894.

147. *Coconino Weekly Sun,* July 5, 1894.

148. *Coconino Weekly Sun,* August 16, 1894.

149. The *thoroughbrace* was a suspension system, in which the carriage was slung above the chassis on long leather slings. It cushioned the ride for both passengers and horses. It was made famous by the Concord coaches, and the article may have been referring to a Concord coach without calling it that.

150. *Coconino Weekly Sun,* August 16, 1894.

151. *Coconino Weekly Sun,* June 7, 1894.

152. *Coconino Weekly Sun,* August 30, 1894. Some writers have claimed that the Grand Canyon stage line carried only passengers, no mail. The fact that Tolfree post office was created implies that the coach did carry mail, for it would have been the only way for regular mail delivery to have occurred at Tolfree.

Also we have quoted comments from two travelers who refer to the carrying of mail by the stage line.

153. *Coconino Weekly Sun,* September 6, 1894. The *Sun* reprinted an article carried in the *Tucson Star* to this effect.

154. *Coconino Weekly Sun,* November 1, 1894.

155. *Coconino Weekly Sun,* November 1, 1894, and November 29, 1894.

156. *Coconino Weekly Sun,* November 29, 1894.

157. *Coconino Weekly Sun,* December 6, 1894, December 13, 1894, and December 20, 1894.

158. Records of Coconino County, Arizona. Recorder's Office. Maps File 1 Map 13 Drawer 29B.

159. *Coconino Sun,* February 28, 1895, and March 14, 1895. Wilcox remained in Flagstaff in the livery business. He suffered a great personal tragedy in 1899 when "membranous croup" killed his two children, Willie and Viola in March 1899. The same week that the children died, a Sheriff's Sale was announced on his home. *Flagstaff Gem,* March 9 and March 16, 1899.

160. Wilson Collection—MS 162. Folder 16. NAU Special Collections, Cline Library.

161. *Coconino Sun,* February 28, 1895.

162. *Coconino Sun,* April 11, 1895.

163. *Coconino Sun,* April 11, 1895.

164. Clipping found in the "Grand Canyon File" at the Sharlot Hall Museum, Prescott. Author and newspaper unknown. Only the date, August 1897, was shown.

165. *Los Angeles Times,* June 2, 1895.

166. The *Sun* carried an article in 1899 that Edith Tolfree was a member of the Junior Class at the School of Oratory at Northwestern University. *Coconino Sun,* April 8, 1899. One wonders what she did with her degree. Edith married M. T. Heavy [or Heavey] in Williams, where the family was then running the Tolfree Hotel [also known as the Parker House]. *Coconino Sun,* September 8, 1900.

167. H. G. Otis, "To the Grand Canyon." *Los Angeles Times,* June 2, 1895.

168. *Coconino Weekly Sun,* May 16, 1895.

169. *Coconino Weekly Sun,* May 23, 1895.

170. *Coconino Weekly Sun,* June 6, 1895.

171. *Coconino Weekly Sun,* June 13, 1895.

172. *Coconino Weekly Sun,* June 6 and June 13, 1895.

173. *Coconino Weekly Sun,* June 13, 1895.

174. *Land of Sunshine.* September 1895. "The Greatest Thing in the World." Charles Lummis. p. 195.

175. *Southwest Illustrated Magazine.* October 1895. "The Grand Canyon of the Colorado." G. A. Neeff. p. 187.

176. J. Curtis Wasson, who took the stage to the Canyon in June 1896, mentioned that the first stop was at Little Spring. Woods. *op. cit.* p. 23.

177. Missouri Bill Klostermeyer was shot to death in May 1895 by another sheep rancher, Gus Mudersbach. *Mountain Living Magazine.* September 1998. "The Death of Missouri Bill." Richard K. Mangum. p. 75. Klostermeyer's widow, Lora, referred to by Neeff, though not by name, married Oscar LeBarron, a sheep rancher, and hotel manager, in November 1896. *Coconino Sun,* November 12, 1896.

178. *Southwest Illustrated Magazine. op. cit.* p. 188.

179. Evidently this was the same Robert A. Ferguson who worked with the Camerons, Pete Berry and others in the construction of the Bright Angel Trail. One wonders what his associates would have thought of his claim that he laid out the trail. Ferguson was also associated in the construction of the Grandview Trail. He did not do his share of the work nor pay his share of expenses, so his interest was forfeited by the Camerons and Berry. Records of Coconino County, Arizona, Book 1 of Promiscuous Records page 97, Forfeiture Notice.

180. *Leslie's Popular Monthly,* June 1896. "In the Grand Canyon of the Colorado." Edith Sessions Tupper. pp. 677-684.

181. *Coconino Weekly Sun,* June 18, 1895.

182. *Coconino Weekly Sun,* September 12, 1895.

183. *Coconino Weekly Sun,* June 13, 1895.

184. *Coconino Weekly Sun,* May 2, 1895.

185. *Coconino Weekly Sun,* March 7, 1895.

186. *Coconino Weekly Sun,* May 9, 1895.

187. *Coconino Weekly Sun,* May 9, 1895. The *Sun* headlined an article: "The New Railroad, Its Success Is Now Assured Beyond Any Doubt."

188. *Coconino Weekly Sun,* June 27, 1895.

189. *Coconino Weekly Sun,* September 5, 1895.

190. *Coconino Weekly Sun,* September 19, 1895; September 26, 1895; October 31, 1895; December 26, 1895.

191. *Coconino Weekly Sun,* August 8, 1895.

192. *Coconino Weekly Sun,* October 31, 1895.

193. *Coconino Weekly Sun,* November 7, 1895.

194. *Coconino Weekly Sun,* December 19, 1895.

195. *Coconino Weekly Sun,* October 17, 1895.

196. *Arizona Champion,* October 16, 1886. Hance published a Notice that he had taken possession of the land about June 15, 1884, locating a home on unsurveyed public land of the United States. He never followed through on this Notice to obtain a Patent. Years later Hance actually did get a Patent, based on a later application, and using a different description, (though covering mostly the same land). It was issued on Feb. 25, 1907. Book 32 of Deeds, page 599, Records of Coconino County, Arizona.

197. United States Revised Statutes of 1878, §2263.

198. Records of Coconino County, Arizona. Book 3 of Deeds page 46.

199. Records of Coconino County, Arizona. Book 32 of Deeds page 599.

200. Michael F. Anderson. *Living at the Edge.* Grand Canyon Association. Grand Canyon, Arizona 1998. p. 64. Anderson asserts that Thurber and Tolfree then built a new cabin and a barn for Hance near the head of the Old Hance Trail. *op. cit.* End Notes to Chapter Three n. 93-96. We believe, however, that Hance built the new cabin months earlier. Otis, *cited above,* stated in his May 29, 1895 article—from information no doubt provided by Hance himself—that Hance built the cabin and his description indicates him living there in May. Edith Tupper's narration also makes the cabin seem to have been well-settled when she visited Hance there in July 1895. Anderson speculates that the old cabin was moved to the head of the trail so that Hance could live in it, but we believe that photographs show that the old cabin remained in place for many seasons and that the new cabin has quite a different appearance from the old, with squared logs and a much more finished look.

201. Hughes, J. Donald. *In the House of Stone and Light.* Grand Canyon Natural History Association. 1978. [This book is a revision of *The Story of Man at Grand Canyon* by Hughes in

1967]. p. 68.

202. Woods. *op. cit.* pp. 82-85.

203. Butchart, Harvey. *Grand Canyon Treks.* La Siesta Press. Glendale, CA. 1976. p. 35.

204. *Coconino Sun,* December 28, 1901.

205. *Ibid.*

206. Anderson. *op. cit.* p. 64.

207. *Coconino Sun,* December 17, 1891. McClure, Marshall and Ashurst were still actively using the Red Canyon Trail in 1895. *Coconino Sun,* August 1, 1895; August 8, 1895;

208. *Coconino Sun,* November 7, 1895.

209. *Coconino Sun,* March 12, 1896.

210. *Coconino Weekly Sun,* December 19, 1895.

211. *Coconino Weekly Sun,* February 13, 1896.

212. *Coconino Weekly Sun,* February 27, 1896.

213. *Coconino Weekly Sun,* March 26, 1896.

214. *Coconino Sun,* April 2, 1896.

215. *Coconino Sun,* April 16, 1896.

216. Anderson. *op. cit.* p. 80-81.

217. Wilson File, MS 162, Folder 11, Special Collections, Cline Library, NAU. Letter from L. H. Tolfree to J. W. Thurber, Feb. 26, 1896, on letterhead of the Mojave Depot Hotel, J. H. Tolfree, proprietor. "Yours of the 24th. received tonight also the pass for Wheeler so he will leave here tomorrow morning for Flagstaff so you ought to see him Saturday morning. Dont you think that the show for getting the Hotel built is pretty slim as no doubt it will take some time to get the permit from Washington.... I am sorry to learn that the water out-look is so bad. I would like to have the Hotel hurried up as there will be no use for me to go out there untill we can have some accommodation to feed the people. I will be pleased to have you come here as soon as possible so we [can] talk the situation over as we have a good deal to attend to and will no doubt have our hands full this coming season...." This letter suggests that Wheeler, Tolfree and Thurber, the trio who had bought Hance's trail rights in November 1895, were still doing business together.

218. Anderson. *op. cit.* p. 89.

219. Wilson File, MS 162, Folder 18, Special Collections, Cline Library, NAU.

220. Higgins, C. A. *Grand Cañon of the Colorado River Arizona.* Santa Fe Railroad, Chicago. 1901 edition. p. 29.

221. Anderson. *op. cit.* p.82.

222. Thurber, Tolfree and Wheeler bought the trail operation from Hance, suggesting some form of partnership or joint venture among the three. However, Thurber acted as if he were the sole owner, and when the Bright Angel was sold to Martin Buggeln in 1901, Thurber was the seller.

223. Yavapai County Records Transcribed to Coconino County. p. 488.

224. MS 25.1, Museum of Northern Arizona. There are two books, a big one and a little one. The small book carries registrations from July 1896 through November 1901.

225. Sutphen. *op. cit.* p. 42.

226. Anderson. *op. cit.* p. 82.

227. Elizabeth Hegemann. *Navaho Trading Days.* University of New Mexico Press. Albuquerque. 1963. p. 39.

228. *Coconino Sun,* June 18, 1896.

229. *Coconino Sun,* July 16, 1896.

230. *Flagstaff Sun-Democrat,* January 14, 1897. An ad for the hotel appears, showing LeBarron as superintendent and Thurber as general manager.

231. *Coconino Sun,* April 2, 1896.

232. *Coconino Sun,* November 5, 1896.

233. *Coconino Sun,* February 25, 1897.

234. *Coconino Sun,* April 16, 1896.

235. *Coconino Sun,* May 28, 1896.

236. *Coconino Sun,* July 30, 1896.

237. *Coconino Sun,* January 16, 1896. Several articles through the year speak of the heavy activities at the mine.

238. *Coconino Sun,* June 18, 1896.

239. Records of Coconino County, Arizona. Book 4 of Deeds, page 110. Deed dated September 11, 1896.

240. GCM. Pete Berry File, Item 14817.

241. Records of Coconino County, Arizona. Book 1 Promiscuous Records, page 95.

242. Wheeler continued to live in the Flagstaff area. He seems to have been accident-prone. In June 1898 he was thrown from his horse and broke two ribs. *Coconino Sun,* June 18, 1898. In 1899, while he was a member of a hose cart team, he fell and the cart ran over him, causing such serious internal injuries that it seemed he would die. *Coconino Sun,* August 12, 1899. He rallied and became Town Marshal of Flagstaff in 1906. He was thrown from his horse at the Flagstaff race track in 1906, suffering head injuries so serious that he lost his mind and was committed to the insane asylum. *Coconino Sun,* August 18, 1906 and October 13, 1906. During his absence another man was appointed to take his place as marshal. Wheeler recovered, returned to Flagstaff, and demanded that his job be restored. *Coconino Sun,* February 14, 1907; February 28, 1907. The City Council yielded to his demand under threats of a lawsuit and re-appointed him, but only as a deputy. *Coconino Sun,* May 2, 1907. He ran for election in 1908 and won, becoming City Marshal again. *Coconino Sun,* May 29, 1908. Shortly afterward, the council agreed to pay him his full back wages. *Coconino Sun,* June 19, 1908.

243. Richmond, Al. *Rails to the Rim.* Grand Canyon Railway. Flagstaff. 1994. p. 16.

244. *Flagstaff Sun-Democrat,* January 14, 1897.

245. *Flagstaff-Sun-Democrat,* January 14, 1897.

246. *Flagstaff-Sun-Democrat,* January 21, 1897.

247. *Flagstaff Sun-Democrat,* February 4, 1897.

248. *Flagstaff Sun-Democrat,* February 4, 1897.

249. *Flagstaff-Sun-Democrat,* March 18, 1897.

250. *Flagstaff Sun-Democrat,* April 15, 1897.

251. *Flagstaff Sun-Democrat,* April 22, and 29, 1897. The office is visible in the 1897 photo. The current owner of the Babbitt Building has repainted the "Grand Cañon Stage Office" lettering in the window, where Thurber's office was, as a contribution to local history.

252. *Flagstaff Sun-Democrat,* April 29, 1897.

253. *Williams News,* April 24, 1897.

254. *Flagstaff Sun-Democrat,* April 8, 1897

255. *Flagstaff Sun-Democrat,* April 29, 1897.

256. *Flagstaff Sun-Democrat,* April 29, 1897

257. *Flagstaff Sun-Democrat,* April 29, 1897.

258. Anderson. *op. cit.* p. 70.

259. GCM. Pete Berry File. Item. #14822.

260. Cameron would become a master of the nuances of the mining laws, using them to tie up hundreds of acres of prime Grand Canyon real estate with a murky brew of bogus, semi-bogus and legitimate mining claims for years, touching off litigation that went through every court in the system. He battled with the Santa Fe, Fred Harvey, the Park Service and everyone else in sight until he ran out of courts in 1926.

261. *Ibid.*

262. Theobald, John and Lillian. *Arizona Territory Post Offices & Postmasters.* Arizona Historical Foundation. Phoenix. 1961. p. 132.

263. *Flagstaff Sun-Democrat,* May 27, 1897.

264. *Flagstaff Sun-Democrat,* May 13, 1897.

265. *Flagstaff Sun-Democrat,* May 27, 1897.

266. *Flagstaff Sun-Democrat,* July 29, 1897

267. *Flagstaff Sun-Democrat,* May 27, 1897.

268. C. M. Funston, the owner of Flagstaff's oldest newspaper, the *Coconino Sun,* closed the paper in 1897 for a few months and took a sabbatical, leaving the field to the upstart *Flagstaff Sun-Democrat,* until he resumed operations in 1898.

269. *Flagstaff Sun-Democrat,* June 10, 1897.

270. *Flagstaff Sun-Democrat,* July 29, 1897. Note that the Phoenix paper was relying on the old schedule, which stated that the stage ran to the Canyon on Mondays, Wednesdays, and Fridays. As we have seen, Thurber was actually running it every day.

271. *Flagstaff Sun-Democrat,* June 10, 1897.

272. *Flagstaff Sun-Democrat,* July 1, 1897.

273. *Flagstaff Sun-Democrat,* August 26, 1897.

274. *Flagstaff Sun-Democrat,* August 26, 1897.

275. *Flagstaff Sun-Democrat,* July 1, 1897.

276. This points out a major difference in the travel experience based on whether a tourist came in from the east or the west. Coming in from the west, the train arrived in Flagstaff in the morning, after the stage had departed, so that a person had most of a day to kill in town. Many used the time to see other sights in the area, such as Walnut Canyon, Oak Creek, Sunset Crater, and so on. Travelers coming from the east arrived in Flagstaff at night, and would usually get on the stage early the next morning.

277. Some writers state that the passengers would get out of the coach to help it get up steep grades, and would even help push it at times. We find no support for this idea. None of the travelers' accounts report such activity. On the contrary, several writers mentioned how they were glad to stretch their legs at stops. The operators negotiated the steep parts—and there were few—by adding additional horses or by mixing in some mules.

278. From personal observation, the authors can attest that petrified wood is scattered about East Cedar Ranch, particularly on the east side of Cedar Ridge, where there is an exposed outcrop of Chinle Formation. The wood is generally not as colorful as the wood found at the Petrified Forest. It consists mostly of small chips, many of which are cream-colored, running to yellow.

279. *Flagstaff Sun-Democrat,* September 9, 1897.

280. *Flagstaff Sun-Democrat,* July 29, 1897.

281. *Flagstaff Sun-Democrat,* July 29, 1897.

282. *Flagstaff Sun-Democrat,* May 13, 1897.

283. *Flagstaff Sun-Democrat,* July 15, 1897.

284. *Flagstaff Sun-Democrat,* July 29, 1897.

285. *Flagstaff Sun-Democrat,* August 12, 1897.

286. *Flagstaff Sun-Democrat,* September 2, 1897. Though the name sounds whimsical, the tie-pickling plant was a significant business operation when completed. It employed thirty men, whose job was to soak railroad ties in a preservative.

287. *Flagstaff Sun Democrat,* August 12, 1897.

288. *Flagstaff Sun Democrat,* September 9, 1897.

289. *Flagstaff Sun Democrat,* September 9, 1897.

290. *Flagstaff Sun Democrat,* October 28, 1897

291. *Flagstaff Sun-Democrat,* September 9, 1897.

292. *Flagstaff Sun-Democrat,* December 2, December 9, and December 16, 1897.

293. *Flagstaff Sun-Democrat,* August 26, 1897.

294. *Flagstaff Sun-Democrat,* October 21, 1897.

295. *Ibid.*

296. *Flagstaff Sun-Democrat,* December 2, 1897.

297. *Flagstaff Sun-Democrat,* September 16, 1897. Oscar LeBarron never rebuilt the hotel. He stayed around Flagstaff for a while, then he and his wife, the former Lora Klostermeyer, moved to Fresno, California. *Coconino Sun,* May 5, 1900.

298. There was also the Hawks Hotel in Flagstaff, just north of the depot; but it was run as a boarding house at the time and did not participate in the Grand Canyon tourism trade.

299. Stoddard and other authors mention arriving in Flagstaff at night in a Pullman and getting on the stage without an intervening stay in a hotel. Apparently this timing worked out for travelers arriving from the east. One of Stoddard's photographs shows his Pullman car sitting on a siding in front of the stage line's office at the depot. Stoddard was awakened at night while sleeping in his Pullman by Flagstaff's fire alarm, a series of pistol shots, and was an eye-witness as the Grand Canyon Hotel burned down. The date of the fire was September 13, 1897.

300. Stoddard, John L. *Stoddard's Lectures.* Vol. 10. Balch Brothers. Boston. 1898. pp. 159-172. Stoddard does not give the date of his visit, but he signed the hotel register at the Canyon on October 5, 1897. His article reveals that he was at the Canyon for many days, covering a span of September 14-October 5 as a minimum. Museum of Northern Arizona, MS 25-1.

301. *Flagstaff Sun-Democrat,* September 23, 1897.

302. *Flagstaff Sun-Democrat,* September 23, 1897.

303. *Flagstaff Sun-Democrat,* November 11, 1897.

304. *Flagstaff Sun-Democrat,* November 4, 1897.

305. *Flagstaff Sun-Democrat,* November 4, 1897.

306. *Coconino Sun,* March 12, 1898.

307. *Coconino Sun,* February 19, 1898.

308. *Coconino Sun,* January 29, 1898.

309. *Coconino Sun,* September 24, 1898.

310. *Flagstaff Gem,* March 10, 1898.

311. *Coconino Sun,* March 12, 1898

312. *Flagstaff Gem,* April 7, 1898. The authors gained considerable insight into the need to stock the relay stations with grain by talking to Roger Hartman, owner and operator of the Lake Mary Stables in Flagstaff. He advised that working horses must be grain-fed, that grass is an insufficient ration for them. Thurber would have needed to supply the relay stations with grain throughout the season—lots of it, since work horses are voracious eaters.

eaters.

313. *Flagstaff Gem,* March 31, 1898.

314. *Flagstaff Gem,* March 24, 1898 and April 14, 1898.

315. *Coconino Sun,* February 26, 1898.

316. *Flagstaff Gem,* April 14, 1898.

317. *Coconino Sun,* March 5, 1898.

318. *Coconino Sun,* May 28, 1898.

319. *Flagstaff Gem,* April 21, 1898.

320. *Mountain Living Magazine.* "Remember the Maine." Richard K. Mangum. December 1998. p. 67.

321. *Coconino Sun,* July 16, 1898.

322. *Coconino Sun,* May 26, 1892.

323. Unknown newspaper. Clipping found in "Grand Canyon File" at Sharlot Hall Museum, Prescott. The date July 1898 is penciled in at the top of the clipping.

324. Holmes, Burton. *Travelogues.* The McClure Company. New York. 1908. pp. 123-124.

325. Holmes. *op. cit.* p. 129.

326. Holmes. *op. cit.* p. 136.

327. Holmes. *op. cit.* p. 137.

328. Holmes. *op. cit.* p. 154.

329. Holmes. *op. cit.* p. 155.

330. Holmes. *op. cit.* p. 156.

331. Holmes. *op. cit.* p. 187.

332. Holmes. *op. cit.* p. 187. We find these two passages enlightening. Holmes, a professional traveler, no doubt prepared himself for his Canyon visit, yet had no idea that Berry had a hotel in the vicinity. He stumbled across it while walking along the rim. This suggests that Berry had little or no advertising or publicity, and may not even have had any signs at the Rim.

333. Holmes. *op. cit.* p. 188.

334. Holmes. *op. cit.* 198.

335. Holmes also had a movie camera and took films to show as an accompaniment to his lectures. The *Coconino Sun* mentioned such a lecture that Holmes gave to an audience of five hundred people in Detroit in 1900. *Coconino Sun,* February 10, 1900.

336. Dysart, Zella. *Summer Sojourn to the Grand Canyon, the 1898 Diary of Zella Dysart,* edited by Mona L. McCroskey. HollyBear Press, Prescott, AZ. p. 47. Some writers have claimed that the Grand Canyon Stage Line carried only passengers, no mail. We believe that this passage shows that the stage did carry mail. It probably also carried supplies, such as canned food, newspapers, books and magazines to those who lived at the Canyon. Zella's older brother, Fred Dysart, had taken the Grand Canyon-Flagstaff Stage Line as a member of the International Order of Grand Templars, a temperance organization, while attending their conference in Flagstaff in 1895. See *Coconino Weekly Sun,* August 29, 1895.

337. Dysart. *op. cit.* p. 47. This is interesting. The authors have wondered how Pete Berry got travelers to go to the Grandview Hotel, which was in full swing by 1898. Thurber, who ran the stage line, owned two competing lodgings—at Thurber's Camp and the Bright Angel Hotel—and would no doubt have steered all the business he could control to his own properties. If Berry relied on such crude means as this signboard, it is no wonder that travelers were ignorant of his presence in the area.

338. Dysart. *op. cit.* p. 47.

339. Dysart. *op. cit.* p. 51.

340. Dysart. *op. cit.* p. 48. This may explain how Hance and William Hull divided the business: Hance's place getting the hotel trade and Hull getting the campers.

341. *Harper's New Monthly Magazine.* No. 579. August 1898. pp. 377-392. "Under the Spell of the Grand Cañon." T. Mitchell Prudden. This makes it even clearer that the stage did not use the Grandview Hotel as its terminus until later.

342. In those days, the noon meal was often called dinner.

343. *Land of Sunshine.* August 1898. "Into the Grand Canyon." Charles Lummis. p. 148.

344. *Diary of Sidney B. Foote.* Museum of Northern Arizona. MS 196. Unpublished. Hance's action was remarkable, considering that he had sold the tourist-use of the trail to Thurber, and that Stella Dysart had reported that the going rate for the use of the trail including guide, gear and animals was five dollars per person. He was probably putting one over on the tenderfeet, whom he considered fair game.

345. *Coconino Sun,* November 5, 1898.

346. *Coconino Sun,* November 5, 1898.

347. *Coconino Sun,* November 19, 1898.

348. *Coconino Sun,* November 19, 1898.

349. *Coconino Sun,* December 3, 1898.

350. *Coconino Sun,* December 24, 1898.

351. *Coconino Sun,* December 24, 1898.

352. *Coconino Sun,* February 4, 1899. The *Sun* was apparently picking up the following story: "Chicago, Jan. 29. The contract for the horseless carriages to be operated by the Santa Fe road between Flagstaff, Ariz., and the Grand Canyon calls for three large coaches, to cost $4,000 each, and six smaller ones. These will be constructed by the Everett King Manufacturing company of this city." Jan. 29, 1899. Source unknown. Clipping found in "Grand Canyon File," Sharlot Hall Museum, Prescott.

353. *Coconino Sun,* February 18, 1899.

354. Source unknown. Clipping found in "Grand Canyon File", Sharlot Hall Museum, Prescott. The *Williams News* claimed that the story was a hoax in another clipping contained in the same file.

355. *Flagstaff Gem,* January 12, 1899.

356. *Flagstaff Gem,* March 23, 1899.

357. *Coconino Sun,* April 8, 1899.

358. *Flagstaff Gem,* April 6, 1899.

359. *Flagstaff Gem,* July 6, 1899.

360. *Flagstaff Gem,* May 4, 1899 and May 11, 1899.

361. *Flagstaff Gem,* June 8, 1899.

362. *Flagstaff Gem,* May 4, 1899.

363. *Flagstaff Gem,* May 4, 1899.

364. *Flagstaff Gem,* June 1, 1899 and in every following issue during the summer.

365. Theobald. *op. cit.* p. 132.

366. *Atlantic Monthly.* December 1899. pp. 816-21. "The Grand Canyon of the Colorado." Harriet Monroe. p. 818.

367. Woods. *op. cit.* p. 126. The *Sun* carried an article in February 1899 to the effect that Woods had embarked on a publishing project, a book on the Grand Canyon based on John Hance's Guest Book. *Coconino Sun,* February 25, 1899. The book was ready in July: *Coconino Sun,* July 1, 1899. It was published, enjoyed good sales has become a Grand Canyon classic, an essential reference work for historians.

368. James, George Wharton. *In and Around the Grand Canyon. 1900.* pp. vii and 126.

369. *Coconino Sun,* April 29, 1899.

370. *Coconino Sun,* April 29, 1899. The "Cameron Trail" could have been a reference either to the Bright Angel Trail or to the Grandview Trail. We believe it referred to the Grandview. Our reason for thinking this is that when Al Doyle guided the first automobile party to the Grand Canyon, they ended up at the Grandview Hotel.

371. *Coconino Sun,* April 15, 1899.

372. *Coconino Sun,* April 29, 1899.

373. *Coconino Sun,* May 13, 1899.

374. *Coconino Sun,* May 13, 1899.

375. *Coconino Sun,* May 20, 1899.

376. *Coconino Sun,* May 27, 1899.

377. *Atlantic. op. cit.*

378. *Catholic World.* December 1899. "The Grand Canyon of the Colorado." Anonymous. The writer also spoke of going from the camp to Bissell's Point, nine miles away. This was the distance from the Grandview Hotel to Bissell's given by Berry. The authors found a printed envelope of Berry's in the GCM giving this distance.

379. Richmond. *op. cit.* p. 14.

380. *Flagstaff Gem,* June 8, 1899.

381. *Coconino Sun,* June 24, 1899.

382. *Coconino Sun,* July 8, 1899.

383. *Coconino Sun,* October 14, 1899.

384. *Coconino Sun,* November 11, 1899.

385. *Coconino Sun,* November 18, 1899.

386. *Coconino Sun,* March 3, 1900.

387. *Coconino Sun,* January 20, 1900.

388. Museum of Northern Arizona, MS 25.1.

389. *Coconino Sun,* March 3, 1900. The *Sun's* account stated that Thurber would put on stages from the end of the railroad about March 15 and that they would run to the Berry hotel, with Thurber in charge of the hotel. The End-of-Track stage did run to the Grandview, but it seems hard to believe that the newspaper was correct about Thurber running Berry's hotel.

390. Richmond. *op. cit.* p. 18.

391. Gerber, Rudy J. *Grand Canyon Railroad.* Primer Publishers. Phoenix. 1990. p. 45.

392. *Flagstaff Gem,* May 10, 1900 and following throughout the summer.

393. *Coconino Sun,* March 31, 1900.

394. *Coconino Sun,* July 14, 1900.

395. *Coconino Sun,* September 8, 1900.

396. *Coconino Sun,* July 7, 1900. While some travelers might have preferred an eleven-hour stage ride, at a cost of $15.00, to a four-hour train-stage ride costing $10.00, their numbers were limited, and the editor was whistling in the dark. The comfort, convenience and cost of the train were obviously going to predominate.

397. *Coconino Sun,* February 3, 1900.

398. Biestman returned to work with the Fred Harvey company and was assigned to manage its restaurant in Gallup, thereafter moving to California in 1901. *Coconino Sun,* July 13, 1901.

399. *Coconino Sun,* March 17, 1900.

400. *Coconino Sun,* June 30, 1900. Tolfree was a professional hotelier, thoroughly familiar with Grand Canyon tourism. The fact that he moved from Flagstaff to Williams may have signaled that the railroad, though still unfinished, was bringing about a shift of the center of tourism from Flagstaff to Williams.

401. *Coconino Sun,* July 7, 1900.

402. *Coconino Sun,* July 28, 1900. Donahue changed the name of his new hotel from the Hotel Flagstaff to the Commercial Hotel in July 1900.

403. *Coconino Sun,* July 14, 1900.

404. *Coconino Sun,* July 14, 1900.

405. *Coconino Sun,* April 21, 1900.

406. *Coconino Sun,* June 16, 1900.

407. *Flagstaff Gem,* July 5, 1900.

408. *Coconino Sun,* July 7, 1900.

409. *Coconino Sun,* July 14, 1900.

410. Richmond. *op. cit.* p. 19.

411. *Coconino Sun,* July 28, 1900; *Flagstaff Gem,* July 26, 1900.

412. GCM. Pete Berry File. The file contains actual tickets issued by the Santa Fe & Grand Canyon Railroad for passage from the End-of-Track to the Grand Canyon via the Bright Angel Stage Line.

413. *Coconino Sun,* July 28, 1900.

414. Berry later wrote a letter to his friend Ralph Cameron in which he stated, "...in 1900 J W Thurber told me that the Santa Fe officials told him to freeze me out and make me walk out of the county...." Sutphen. *op. cit.* p. 53.

415. *Coconino Sun,* August 25, 1900.

416. *Coconino Sun,* June 30, 1892.

417. *Coconino Sun,* September 8, 1900.

418. *Coconino Sun,* August 11, 1900.

419. Richmond. *op. cit.* p. 20.

420. Richmond. *op. cit.* p. 17.

421. Richmond. *op. cit.* p. 22.

422. GCM. Pete Berry File. Item #14850. The curt language of the letter was: "Dear Sir, By order of Mr. Jno. J. Byrne, G. P. A. This is to advise you that hereafter the tickets issued by this office reading over stage line to the Grand Canyon will be good only over the stage line run by Mr. J. W. Thurber." Date October 6, 1900.

423. Museum of Northern Arizona, MS 25-1.

424. Wilson Collection—MS 162. Special Collections. Northern Arizona University. Folder 5.

425. *Ibid.* Folder 11.

426. It would have been a common business practice for Berry to pay Thurber some kind of a commission or percentage for each guest delivered by the Grand Canyon-Flagstaff Stage Line to the Grandview, though we have seen nothing to confirm that Berry and Thurber had such an arrangement.

427. Dillman, Albert A. Interview. July 21, 1977. Museum of Northern Arizona. MS 259. Albert Dillman was the son of Gus and Lina Dillman, who ran the first stage stop from 1892-1895. He saw the result of the sudden termination of the Grand Canyon-Flagstaff Stage Line at East Cedar Ranch: "...when they quit, they just packed their suitcases and that was it. They left everything and we learned later on that people went out there and helped themselves. My brother rode out there to investigate, and a lot of the

stuff was gone—all the beautiful linen. He gathered up a lot of the dishes and everything and packed the odds and ends and things people didn't want, tied it on the back of his saddle, and took it on home. We still have some of it. The dishes had an oak leaf shaped out with a couple little leaves on it."

Mr. Dillman retold a family legend which has been repeated uncritically by various authors, namely that Teddy Roosevelt was a passenger on the stage line and gave Mrs. Dillman a silver dollar for a snack, which she treasured as a keepsake. It seems cruel to spike such a nice story, but Roosevelt's movements were well documented. He was first in Arizona in 1903, when he went to the Grand Canyon by train. He was also here in 1911 and 1913. He could not have taken the stage line to the Grand Canyon in any of these years.

One of the authors, Richard Mangum, remembers that there were still a cabin and shed at Little Spring until the mid-1960s, when the Forest Service tore them down. The hotel corporation formed by Flagstaff businessmen at the inception of the stage line built the "hotel" at East Cedar Ranch, so Thurber sacrificed nothing by leaving it. It is not clear whether the corporation or Thurber erected the buildings at Little Spring, though we would guess that Thurber built them. It seems clear that Thurber built the kitchen-dining room building at Thurber's Camp.

428. There is no record in the Recorder's Office of Coconino County to show that Thurber sold his trail rights to anyone.

429. *Coconino Sun,* December 15, 1900.

430. GCM. Pete Berry File. Letter from Geo. A. Reed to Lemuel A. Garrison, Acting Superintendent of Grand Canyon National Park, August 15, 1948. Reed moved to the Grand Canyon, at the old Hull Tank Cabin and Hull Ranch, in 1903. Speaking of Hance's property, he wrote, "At one time a man named Thurber used this cabin for a stage station and I think he really built it but Cap claimed the land and later, in my time, did live in it...."

431. Sutphen. *op. cit.* p. 44.

432. GCM. Bert Cameron Interview.

433. *Coconino Sun,* June 22, 1901.

434. Higgins, C. A. *Grand Cañon of the Colorado River Arizona.* Santa Fe Railroad, Chicago 1893. Revised periodically after the first edition. The Announcement in question was added to the 1901 edition. In 1901 the Santa Fe changed its spelling protocols. It began using the word "Canyon" instead of "Cañon," and referred to the "Grand Canyon of Arizona," instead of the "Grand Canyon of the Colorado River in Arizona." *Prescott Journal-Miner,* September 1901.

435. Sanborn Maps 1901. These maps, periodically prepared by a fire insurance rating service, show the building on the 1892 map and the 1896 map. It is missing on the 1901 map.

436. *Coconino Sun,* March 23, 1901. Charles Miller, who had managed the Bright Angel in 1899 and 1900, died of pneumonia in Los Angeles before the season started. *Coconino Sun,* January 26, 1901.

437. *Coconino Sun,* February 2, 1901.

438. *Coconino Sun,* March 2, 1901.

439. *Coconino Sun,* March 30, 1901.

440. *Coconino Sun,* April 13, 1901.

441. *Coconino Sun,* June 22, 1901.

442. *Coconino Sun,* May 4, 1901.

443. In December 1901 it was reported that Thurber, a resident of Long Beach, had a contract for grading fourteen miles of electric lines near Los Angeles. *Coconino Sun,* December 7, 1901.

444. *Coconino Sun,* May 25, 1901.

445. *Coconino Sun,* June 1, 1901.

446. *Coconino Sun,* June 8, 1901. In August a guest who had stayed at the Grandview came into Flagstaff and told the *Sun* that "tourist travel to that point is good." *Coconino Sun,* August 17, 1901.

447. *Coconino Sun,* January 19, 1901.

448. *Coconino Sun,* February 2, 1901.

449. *Coconino Sun,* April 20, 1901.

450. *Coconino Sun,* June 22, 1901.

451. *Coconino Sun,* July 20, 1901.

452. Richmond. *op. cit.* p. 21.

453. Richmond. *op. cit.* p. 22.

454. Richmond. *op. cit.* p. 20.

455. *Coconino Sun,* July 6, 1901.

456. *Ibid.* Tolfree left Williams but was uncertain about where to relocate. He considered taking over the management of the newly opened Copper Queen Hotel in Bisbee. *Coconino Sun,* August 24, 1901. This did not occur, and he then hinted that he might come back to Flagstaff. *Coconino Sun,* September 28, 1901. He and his wife wound up moving to Pomona, California, to manage the Palomares Hotel. *Coconino Sun,* November 2, 1901. Tolfree returned to Flagstaff in 1902 as manager of the Weatherford Hotel, went to Tucson for a time, returned to Flagstaff and while managing the Commercial Hotel in 1905, committed suicide.

457. *Coconino Sun,* June 29, 1901.

458. *Coconino Sun,* October 26, 1901. In this article, John Marshall was added to the list of owners. The article also stated that the sellers had had an earlier sale for $25,000 in the making, but the Panic of '93 had thwarted it. Hance later told listeners that he had used his share of the money to go to San Francisco where he spent the loot freely in an epic binge, about which he had no regrets.

459. *Coconino Sun,* November 16, 1901. In 1904, Hance's authority to act as agent for the mine was revoked, and the authors assume that his tenure as manager was canceled at the same time. Coconino Sun, April 30, 1904.

460. Good, John. *Copper—A Guide to Grandview Trail and Horseshoe Mesa.* Grand Canyon Natural History Association. Grand Canyon. 1985. p. 16. Coconino Sun, August 24, 1901.

461. *Ibid.*

462. *Coconino Sun,* October 12, 1901.

463. Good. *op. cit.*

464. *Coconino Sun,* January 25, 1902.

465. *Arizona and the West.* Spring 1978 pp. 41-64 and Summer 1978 pp. 155-172. "Ralph H. Cameron and the Grand Canyon." Douglas H. Strong. p. 45.

466. Richmond. *op. cit.* p. 39.

467. Richmond. *op. cit.* p. 41.

468. GCM. Promotional card in Pete Berry File. This card was printed for the season of 1901-1902. Berry advertised his hotel rates as $2.00 per day, and offered saddle animals, guides and carriage drives along the Rim for an extra charge.

469. *Coconino Sun,* November 9, 1901.

470. *Coconino Sun,* November 16, 1901.

471. *Coconino Sun,* November 9, 1901.

472. *Coconino Sun,* December 14, 1901. To find out what actually happened the reader is referred to our chapter on autos to the Grand Canyon.

473. *Coconino Sun,* December 28, 1901.

474. There would still be some die-hard and rear guard action. The *Sun,* in its final issue of the year, December 28, 1901, a special edition devoted to promoting the town and people of Flagstaff, gave considerable space to the wonders of the Grand Canyon. The editor, with more optimism than realism, wrote,

"To reach the Canyon the tourist has now two alternatives. He may go by rail via Williams, or he may go by stage or wagon. Of course, if he choose the latter method, he will make his start from Flagstaff, and if he wishes to enjoy the finest trip in the world, he must go in no other way and from no other point."

His comment about going by stage is not understood. We know that the official Thurber-Santa Fe line was no longer running in 1901. It is possible that some entrepreneur stepped into the breach and opened a little line, though there is no mention of such a thing happening in the paper.

475. Hughes, J. Donald. *In the House of Stone and Light.* Grand Canyon Natural History Association. 1978. [This book is a revision of *The Story of Man at Grand Canyon* by Hughes in 1967]. p. 57.

Baedeker's Guide to the United States

This map, nicely done by German cartographers, shows the situation shortly after the railroad was finished. While it is generally accurate, the map perpetuates some outdated information. It shows the Eastern Route curling back to the south to join the Western Route near Little Spring, something it had not done since 1894. It also shows the road going by Red Horse Spring, something else outmoded by the time of the railroad

This map was drawn for the 1897 bike run to the Canyon from Flagstaff by C. H. Coble and W. H. Power. Both were members of the Coconino Cycling Club. Power was a professional surveyor. While the scale of the map was not given, the proportions seem correct. Both the Western and Eastern Routes are depicted. The points on the Western Route are well-known and easy to locate on the ground today, except for Morse Well at the 64 mile point. The Eastern Route, however, contains some place names that have become lost, such as Hell's Half Acre and the Garden of Eden.

We believe that we have located these.

At the Canyon itself, the points are of special interest, as the locations of Thurber's Camp and the surroundings are well shown.

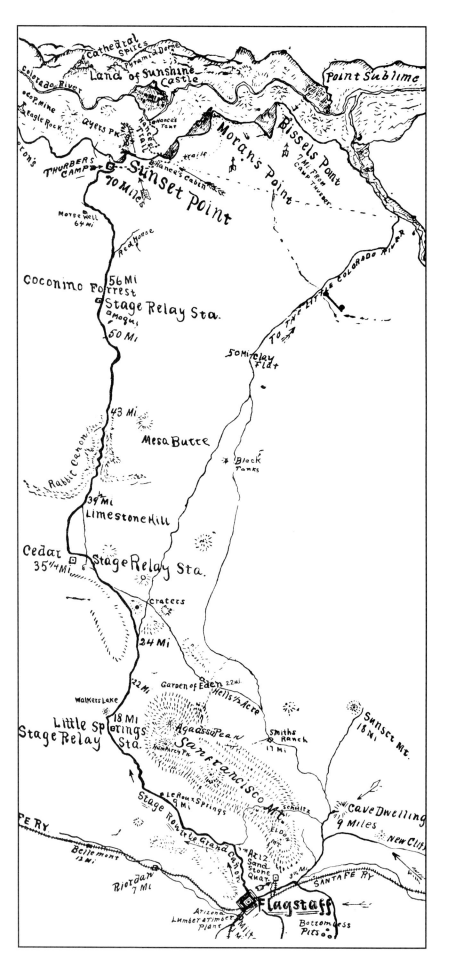

The Coconino Cycling Club at Thurber's Camp,
Grand Canyon, 1896.—Land of Sunshine Magazine

Bicycles

The bicycle reached Flagstaff in 1894. The first newspaper article to mention bicycles in Flagstaff related that E. A Sliker and C. H. Coble rode their cycles to Oak Creek and back in one day.[1] In July 1894 the newspaper noted that Dr. P. G. Cornish was visiting his patients on a bike, including a twenty-five mile round-tripper to Bellemont.[2] By August the paper stated that even the ladies had taken up the sport.[3] By October 1894 the *Sun* opined, "Bicycling is becoming quite a popular fad in Flagstaff, as is evidenced by the number of riders seen on the streets of a Sunday."[4]

The first reported bicycle trip to the Grand Canyon took place in August 1894, and was made by a "bicycle aggregation" of six Flagstaff residents and two men from Albuquerque, who left town at 5:00 a.m. and arrived at the South Rim at 7:00 p.m.[5] This seems to have been an informal event put together by enthusiasts with no official backing and no publicity. The participants apparently enjoyed it so much that they decided to repeat the adventure the following year and to organize themselves and promote the event to the public so as to make it a big event.

In May 1895 seventeen Flagstaff cyclists joined the Phoenix branch of the League of American Wheelmen, allowing them to participate in sanctioned events. The members included many prominent Flagstaff men, whose names historians will recognize:

J. M. Brannen, E. S. Clark, E. A. Sliker, C. Goodchild, F. W. Sisson, C. H. Coble, T. J. Moyer, Harry Cullinan, R. W. Bell, E. E. Ellinwood, W. S. Coffin, Dr. P. G. Cornish, M. J. Riordan, H. R. Davis, A. B. Crawford, Charles Canall and S. T. Elliott.[6]

Flagstaff biking enthusiasts made the second annual run to the Grand Canyon on August 22, 1895. To the disappointment of the Flagstaff bikers, only five riders turned out for the trip: J. M. Aitken and F. D. Myers of Prescott; L. L. Ferrall of Williams; C. H. Coble and T. B. Bell of Flagstaff.[7] They had a bad time on the way to the Canyon, the *Sun* reporting:

The trip to the canyon was a hard one as the riders got caught in a heavy rain storm and the road was muddy. The return trip was made in seven hours. The cyclometer makes the distance to the Grand Canyon 72 miles. A number of bicyclists will make the trip to the canyon some time next month.[8]

The reference to a number of bicyclists making the trip in September is tantalizing, as there is no account of any other group trip in 1895. Perhaps the newspaper was in error.

Land of Sunshine

The Coconino Cycling Club in town

In January 1896 Flagstaff cyclists created the Coconino Cycling Club, with F. W. Sisson, President; Porter W. Fleming First vice-president; S. T. Elliott, Second vice-president; Thomas Bell, Secretary-treasurer; C. H. Coble, Captain; Dr. P. G. Cornish, First lieutenant; J. M. Brannen, Second lieutenant; and W. H. Switzer, Color bearer.[9] The group had a "cozy clubroom" in the Bank Hotel and met every Monday night.[10] The club took the organization of the annual Grand Canyon run under its wing and immediately began preparations for the third edition, determined that they would organize it properly and make it an important event. Club members prepared press releases and convinced newspapers to print them; long accounts of the forthcoming run were published. They also printed and distributed circulars over a wide area. The Atlantic & Pacific Railroad—no doubt sensing that energetic promotion of the event might bring scores of cyclists to Flagstaff over its rail system—helped with advertising.[11]

The advertising campaign seemed successful, because the club received many inquiries in response to it.[12] Late in July 1896, C. H. Coble and E. A. Sliker made a scouting run to the Canyon using the Eastern Route, leaving Flagstaff at 6:00 a.m. and reaching the Canyon at 7:00 p.m. They measured the road with cyclometers and took note of important points along the way. Later, members erected signs at those points. Coble used the information to draw the map seen on page 74.[13]

Expecting a big turnout, club members made plans to divide the riders into three sections, each section led by a Flagstaff cyclist who had made the trip. In a front-page article, the *Sun* set out the particulars:

Wednesday morning [August 19, 1896] the start will be made for the run to the canyon. The following is the schedule of Coconino Cycling Club run to the Grand Canyon:

	FIRST SECTION	SECOND SECTION	THIRD SECTION
Lv Flagstaff	6:00 a.m.	6:00 a.m.	6:00 a.m.
Ar Garden of E	8:00 a.m.	8:30 a.m.	9:00 a.m.
Ar Cedar Valley	9:30 a.m.	10:15 a.m.	10:45 a.m.
Lv Cedar Valley	10:30 a.m.	11:15 a.m.	11:45 a.m.
Ar Moqui	1:00 p.m.	2:15 p.m.	3:30 p.m.
Ar Tolfree	4:30 p.m.	6:00 p.m.	7:30 p.m.

First Section, Coble and Jasper. Second, Elliott and Clark. Third, Sisson, Moyer and Cornish.

The return run the time will be shortened two hours.

The club has had handsome ribbon badges prepared for presentation to all visitors, to be retained as souvenirs of the run.[14]

In spite of all their efforts to bring in large numbers of riders, club members were disappointed by the turnout. While the organizers expected about sixty out-of-town riders, based on what they had been told by prospective participants, only seven appeared, three from Gallup, three from Albuquerque and one from Wingate. Six Flagstaff riders (the section leaders) took part.[15] The trip was a hard one, as a heavy rain storm caught the riders at Moqui Station. The rain made the road so muddy that six participants dropped out and took the stagecoach to Hance's Camp (Tolfree). Charles Canall of Flagstaff suffered a broken chain and wound up pushing his bike fourteen miles to Thurber's Camp (Tolfree). The next two days the group enjoyed themselves with free time at the Canyon, including a hike down the Grandview Trail to see the caves, then had a pleasant ride back to town in dry weather.[16]

Sheep man Abizer J. (Jack) LeBarron had a dangerous experience at the time of the Grand Canyon run in 1896. Setting off by himself, he took the wrong fork at the Tuba City Road junction, not realizing his mistake until he had reached the Little Colorado River, by which time he was faint with thirst, only to find that the river water was undrinkable. He might have died except for being rescued by Navajos. Coconino Cycling Club members soon remedied the problem by erecting a sign post at the junction.[17]

In 1897 the Coconino Cycling Club, undaunted by the meager turnout in 1896, began preparations early for the fourth annual run, to take place on September 11. In April, they had the *Sun* print the announcement shown here.

Advertisement prepared by the Coconino Cycling Club for the 1897 event.

Land of Sunshine Magazine

MNA MS 26-38a

A view of the Eastern Route, showing the terrain that cyclists encountered. In the cinder hills north of the Peaks, the land was easy going for several miles.

The *Sun* reported, "The officers of the club will spare neither labor nor expense in making this run a success and an enjoyable affair to visiting wheel men."[18]

The club produced as much publicity as possible to disseminate the news and arouse the interest of Western bikers. The preliminary results looked hopeful. In August the *Sun* reported that the run was "...exciting the attention of a considerable number of wheelmen from different parts of the county...." and, "It is expected that this run will be participated in by a large delegation of visiting wheelmen."[19]

Club members even persuaded Coconino County to fix the road. The *Sun*, on August 26, 1897, reported:

> Road overseer Anderson has just completed the work of clearing out the malapai that studded a long stretch of the road to the Grand Canyon, and that thoroughfare is now as smooth as a boulevard.[20]

The road improvements were tested and a record was established when for the first time a woman made the bicycle ride from Flagstaff to the Grand Canyon, the *Sun* gave the interesting details:

> Miss Edith Brooks of Phoenix, who is spending the summer here, stopping at the residence of W. H. Power, accomplished a feat last week never before attempted by a woman—a bicycle ride to the Grand Canyon of the Colorado. She accompanied Mr. and Mrs. W. H. Power, Miss Addine Bury, Miss Ida Warren, Dr. E. S. Miller and J. W. Power on their trip, they being equipped with a double-seated covered spring-wagon and saddle ponies. The party occupied two days in going and in coming. Miss Brooks made the seventy-two-mile trip with comparative ease and was frequently compelled to slow up in her speed to allow the wagon to catch up. She says that the trip can easily be accomplished in a day and believes she can do it in that time. Miss Brooks is an enthusiast on cycling and in Phoenix is a familiar figure at the cycle runs. The ride to the Grand Canyon is in reality a trip that taxes the endurance of our best male bicyclists on account of the grade encountered. The road, however, is excellent.[21]

The account of the much-ballyhooed 1897 ride is missing from the newspaper files, but it must be assumed that the experience was similar to that of 1896, when many riders expressed interest in making the trip, but only a few appeared. We assume that the event was a failure because the club never again sponsored a run from Flagstaff to the Grand Canyon. The 1897 event was the end of the Flagstaff to Grand Canyon annual bicycle runs, which occurred in 1894, 1895, 1896 and 1897.

In recent years with the popularity of mountain bikes, runs from Flagstaff to the Grand Canyon have become common. The authors accompanied the ride in 1994, sponsored by the Museum of Northern Arizona. The trip started from a point about eleven miles north of town, so that it was only about sixty miles long. Riders spent a night on the road. All of the participants had modern bikes with multiple-speeds, high-tech equipment and van furnishing full support. Even so, it was a tough trip for most participants, with some unable to finish. Our ancestors were a hardy lot. They were making a full seventy-two mile trip in one day, with one-speed machines and primitive tires that frequently went flat. Hats off to those pioneers!

MNA MS 26-36.a

Cyclists in a logged area outside Flagstaff, circa 1902

Endnotes

1. *Coconino Sun,* May 17, 1894.
2. *Coconino Sun,* July 5, 1894.
3. *Coconino Sun,* August 2, 1894.
4. *Coconino Sun,* October 18, 1894.
5. *Coconino Sun,* August 30, 1894.
6. *Coconino Sun,* May 16, 1895, June 20, and July 30, 1895.
7. *Coconino Sun,* August 22, 1895.
8. *Coconino Sun,* August 29, 1895.
9. *Coconino Sun,* January 23, 1896.
10. *Coconino Sun,* June 25, 1896.
11. *Coconino Sun,* May 21, May 28, and June 11, 1896.
12. *Coconino Sun,* June 25, 1896.
13. *Coconino Sun,* July 30, 1896.
14. *Coconino Sun,* August 13, 1896.
15. *Coconino Sun,* August 20, 1896.
16. *Coconino Sun,* August 27, 1896.
17. *Coconino Sun,* August 20, 1896.
18. *Coconino Sun,* April 29, 1897.
19. *Coconino Sun,* August 5, 1897.
20. *Coconino Sun,* August 26, 1897.
21. *Coconino Sun,* August 26, 1897.

Holmes Travelogues

Bicycle seen in the forest outside of Flagstaff in 1898. The lovely, open forest filled with prime first-growth Ponderosa pine is well shown here, as is the condition of this typical road

Holmes Travelogues

These cyclists were seen by Holmes at Yellowstone in the 1890s, but are typical of the day. Perhaps members of the Coconino Cycling Club looked something like this when they were on the stage road

First car from Flagstaff (or anywhere else) to the Grand Canyon , January 6, 1902. This picture was posed at the Grandview Hotel after Pete Berry's horses towed the disabled vehicle to the hotel. The undaunted travelers posed in it the following day. Seated in the back are Al Doyle and Thomas Chapman. At the driver's tiller Oliver Lippincott, flanked by Winfield Hogaboom. Their journey was a trip from Hell

AUTOMOBILES

By 1899 automobiles were starting to make an impact on the American scene, though few people in Arizona had ever seen one. Under these conditions it is remarkable that the Santa Fe Railroad would consider running an auto stage line from Flagstaff to the Grand Canyon, but that is what it did. It commissioned car maker Everett-King of Chicago to construct three specially designed horseless carriages for the purpose, then changed the contract to ten. The design was for large "carettes" capable of seating eighteen people, twelve inside and eight on top, propelled by a fourteen-horsepower engine.[1] For some unstated reason, the project was aborted, and it may have been a hoax.[2] Nonetheless, the idea was a harbinger of things to come. To those whose eyes were unblinded by centuries of tradition, it was obvious that the days of the stagecoach were numbered, even in the rural West.

Although the Santa Fe's plan fizzled out, the idea of an auto line from Flagstaff to the Grand Canyon was still very much alive. By late 1899 Flagstaff residents were alarmed by the fact that the Santa Fe and Grand Canyon Railroad had actually put down several miles of track, and that Flagstaff was in danger of losing its long-held role as Gateway to the Grand Canyon. An auto line held out the promise of competing with the railroad. It also had the potential to be a money-maker for anyone who invested in it.

The next development in the saga occurred the following year, in 1900, when Samuel E. Faroat and his wife came to Flagstaff from New York hoping that the climate would improve his health.[3] In the summer of 1900 Faroat looked over the tourism situation and came up with an auto-stage proposition which he pitched to Flagstaff residents. He first advanced the notion of creating a corporation for the purpose of purchasing automobiles and establishing a tourist line, not only to the Grand Canyon but to other points of interest around Flagstaff.[4] This apparently failed to generate any enthusiasm and was never mentioned again. In July 1900 Faroat decided to take another approach, announcing that he would create the auto stage line himself, asking only that Flagstaff residents pledge to buy one hundred advance round-trip tickets at fifteen dollars each. With this guarantee, he said he would go East, buy an auto that would seat six persons, bring it to Flagstaff and give it a test run to the Grand Canyon. He intended to have a mechanic at the factory take the car apart and reassemble it in his presence so that he would know how to repair it, as there were no auto mechanics in Flagstaff.[5] He figured that the vehicle would cost two thousand dollars, meaning that he was risking about five hundred dollars of his own money, plus expenses; so he was no Fly-by-Night promoter.[6] His proposition enlisted the support of two well-known local men, John G. Verkamp and Ed I. Gale, who canvassed Flagstaff businessmen and secured promises for the purchase of the one hundred tickets in one day of asking.[7] With the initial financing secured, Faroat left for Chicago.[8]

While he was in Chicago, the home office of the Santa Fe Pacific Railroad, Faroat visited with Santa Fe officials and was able to interest them in the project.[9] The Santa Fe would not invest any money in the line, but it would sell combination tickets, so that rail passengers could buy a ticket anywhere, ride the Santa Fe to Flagstaff and then transfer to the auto stage line for the Grand Canyon.[10] It should be remembered that at this time the Santa Fe did not own the spur line to the Grand Canyon from Williams and was still sponsoring the old horse-drawn stage line from Flagstaff.

After this promising stopover in Chicago, Faroat went on to New York City, where he talked about automobiles and was advised that the best vehicle for his purpose was made by the Haynes-Apperson Company in Kokomo, Indiana.[11] He then ordered a car from Haynes-Apperson, equipped with a twelve-horsepower engine and capable of carrying seven passengers. It was to be built especially for mountain roads. The company even promised to send a man out with the car and accompany Faroat on the test drive from Flagstaff to the Canyon. Faroat expected that the trip would take eight hours, possibly even six. The car was due to arrive in early October, with the test-run to take place immediately thereafter.[12]

GCM 16413

Before long, stunt shots like this were common

Upon his return to Flagstaff, and anticipating that everything would go well, Faroat put tickets on sale in August. They were available at the Western Union office were numbered, with purchasers being guaranteed rides in the order of their ticket numbers.[13]

While he was awaiting the arrival of the car, Faroat went out and inspected the roads.[14] Faroat did not intend to use the old stagecoach roads, either the Western or the Eastern Route; instead, he would start on a county road, then switch to a new road that Al Doyle had laid out,which never joined the stage road at any point. This new path was touted as being twelve miles shorter than the stagecoach road.[15] This route was generally called the Mudersbach Road, as it went past the Mudersbach Ranch in the area of Kendrick Peak.[16] In late summer Al Doyle took eight men out into the field to work on the road, assisted by Coconino County maintenance crews. It was reported that Doyle was building fifty miles of new road and that the county was graveling its part of the road.[17] Faroat filed a Toll Road Certificate for the route on October 30, 1900.[18]

The automobile arrived late in October. The editor of the *Gem* was treated to a ride around town and wrote,

> Samuel Faroat received an automobile the first of the week. We had the pleasure of a ride on it over the streets and we pronounce it first-class in every respect. The automobile has a capacity of eight besides the conductor. In a week or ten days Mr. Faroat will make a trip on it to the Grand Canyon. It is evident now to those who doubted it at the start, that the automobile line to the Grand Canyon will be a success.

> Mr. Faroat is a pusher and by spring he will have the line fully equipped, and will also have an automobile at this place to convey passengers to points of interest near Flagstaff. A town or city without automobiles is not in it. The Skylight City will soon be the queen city of Arizona.[19]

Unfortunately for Faroat, the factory did not send a mechanic along with the car as promised, so after taking his backers for a spin around town, Faroat parked the vehicle in George Babbitt's garage, awaiting the mechanic.[20] The mechanic arrived in mid-November and vowed that he would remain in town until he had trained some local resident in the arcane art of repairing and maintaining the automobile.[21] That was well and good, but by this time it was too late in the season to think of making a trip to the Canyon. Winter was setting in.

Faroat realized that he could not start the operation of the line in 1900, so loaded the vehicle on a rail car and he sent it to Phoenix, where he planned to spend the winter. He vowed that he would return in the spring of 1901 to start operations.[22]

At the beginning of 1901, Flagstaff residents were keenly interested in having an auto stage line, for at the end of 1900, the horse-drawn line ceased operating. The Santa Fe issued an official Announcement at the beginning of 1901 stating—among other things— that:

> The tri-weekly stage line heretofore operated between Flagstaff and the Grand Cañon has been discontinued.
>
> The trip is now made from Williams, Ariz., a town on the main line of the Santa Fe Route, thirty-four miles west of Flagstaff.
>
> It is proposed to operate an automobile line between Flagstaff and Grand Cañon, of which due announcement will be made later.[23]

There was a danger that the tourist business would be lost to Williams, the terminus of the railroad to the Grand Canyon. The rails had not reached the Canyon yet, and it seemed that the spur line was sputtering to a stop due to financial troubles, so there was still hope that a well-run auto line would furnish stiff competition and keep Flagstaff viable as the Gateway. With Santa Fe support, it was just possible that Flagstaff would keep its tourist business, which had become vital to the town's economy.

In February 1901, Flagstaff newspapers began tooting the horn for the auto line. The *Gem* reprinted the following article from the *Needles Eye:*

> Great is the automobile! It has invaded Arizona. It will compete with the railroad and supplant the stage as a means of reaching the Grand Canyon of Arizona.
>
> If present plans are consummated, passengers can leave the Santa Fe route transcontinental train at Flagstaff, Ariz., and ride over to the Grand Canyon, about sixty miles distant, on a $3,000 automobile, built to seat nine persons. It is expected that the distance will be covered in seven to eight hours.
>
> The journey will be a delightful one, passing for ten miles across open prairie, then for twenty miles through a dense pine forest in full view of the San Francisco mountains, and ending with thirty miles over a slightly rolling country.
>
> The roadway is being improved, so that it will be an ideal course for automobilists. The novelty of a ride in this newest of new machines, more than a mile up to the sky, will serve to call attention anew to the Grand Canyon side trip, already built from Williams almost to the rim of the "Titan of Chasms": —*Needles (Cal.) Eye.*[24]

In April Faroat and his wife came back to Flagstaff from Phoenix and announced that they would soon have the auto line in full swing.[25] A couple of weeks later, Faroat took a job as a salesman for the Babbitt Brothers' Department Store.[26]

The weather was allowing the travel season to open just then, but it was not a good time to begin a new tourist venture from Flagstaff to the Grand Canyon because of what was happening in Williams. The Santa Fe and Grand Canyon Railroad, which had been forced into receivership by creditors, was still running trains to Coconino Siding, some ten miles short of the Canyon, and had been mired in legal proceedings for months. But in the summer of 1901, one could see that the litigation was about to end, and those in the know were cer-

This reenactment in the 1950s attempted to capture the spirit of early motoring to the Grand Canyon

tain that the Santa Fe Pacific Railroad would buy the Grand Canyon railway. If this happened, it was unlikely that the Santa Fe would back the auto line from Flagstaff, instead dedicating all its resources to the rail spur. This is exactly what happened. The Santa Fe bought the major assets of the defunct railroad on July 18, 1901 and immediately began to rebuild and extend the railroad. (See the History chapter of this book for details).

Faroat's auto line never materialized. He never even made a test drive from Flagstaff to the Grand Canyon. The Flagstaff newspapers fell silent about Faroat from May until November 1901, when it was reported:

> S. E. Faroat and wife left Tuesday for San Jose, Cal. Mr. Faroat came here two years ago, for the benefit of his health, which he has fully recovered, and goes to California for the purpose of engaging in business.[27]

No sooner had Faroat left town than Oliver Lippincott, a Los Angeles resident, appeared in Flagstaff and announced that he would drive an automobile from Flagstaff to the Grand Canyon at Christmas time. He made the bold announcement that his car was being shipped into Flagstaff by rail and that when it arrived he would make the drive to the Canyon in from three to four hours. Again, as with Faroat, Lippincott expected that the drive would launch a regular auto stage from Flagstaff to the Grand Canyon.[28]

Lippincott was accompanied by Winfield Hogaboom, a journalist friend, who wrote several published articles about the adventure. In one of these articles he mentioned Faroat's attempt:

> The people of Flagstaff hailed the advent of the automobile with delight and did everything they could to help. But the man never made the attempt. He laid plans for the trip on many different occasions, and just at the last moment he always discovered that something was wrong with his machine, and postponed the trial. At length he loaded his little auto onto a flatcar and went away with it, and the people of Flagstaff never saw him any more.[29]

Lippincott's venture was on an entirely different footing: he had the backing of an auto manufacturer, the American Bicycle Company—maker of the Toledo steam-driven automobile, which thought that the trip would be good publicity for the durability and reliability of its cars, and might lead to a profitable Grand Canyon tourism sideline.[30]

It was Lippincott who came up with the idea and sold it to the maker of the Toledo. Lippincott was an old Grand Canyon hand. A professional photographer, he had been to the Canyon on many occasions, had produced photos used by the Santa Fe in its advertising and had published an entire book of Grand Canyon images, called *Glimpses of the Grand Canyon of the Colorado*.[31]

The car was not shipped to Flagstaff in time to make the run to the Canyon by Christmas, but Lippincott confidently stated that he would make the test drive by year's end. He also gave the details of the vehicle, which were pretty impressive:

> The machine which is to be used in testing the practicability of this represents the very latest type of automobile construction. From bell to whistle it is a perfect locomotive. Its engines are 10-horse power high speed marine engines, copies after the United States torpedo boat type, fitted with water coil and flash boilers.

> There is a storage capacity for thirty gallons of oil and fifty-seven gallons of water. The water reservoir is filled by a patent siphon operated by the engine's own steam. Its speed test, which was made between Toledo and Detroit, is forty—two miles an hour under 175 pounds of steam. The tires of the machine are four inches in width, with solid rubber an inch and a half in thickness.

> The weight of this powerful machine, ready for the start, is about 2,200 pounds, and mud, snow or ice cannot seriously impede its progress.

MNA

Even in the days of the automobile, when the trip from Flagstaff to the Grand Canyon could be made in a few hours, some travelers liked to camp overnight along the way, such as this early motorist. His dog liked car travel so much that he stayed in the seat even after camp was pitched

AHS-PM 22-6

Early autoists had to be ready for anything

MNA 64.1095

Even as cars improved, the early roads took their toll

MNA 72.542

More road hazards

Back of the dashboard is the air gauge and marine clock. On the right driving wheel is a cyclometer recording distances traveled, so arranged by an electrical contrivance as to register each mile and the time in which it is made. It registers time of all stops made for renewing fuel or water. On the front is a headlight twelve inches in diameter of 200 candle-power, lighted with acetylene gas.

The chauffeur manages forward and backward movements and entire action of the machine with a single small lever at the side of the seat. The engines can be reversed with absolute safety at high speed. A double friction bearing brake will bring the vehicle to a stop at once. Three people can be accommodated on the front seat, while the trailer, which is a part of the machine itself, will accommodate three more.[32]

If successful, the backer would organize a transit company headquartered in Flagstaff and put three big steam coaches on the line, making round trips to the Grand Canyon and back in a day. Each coach would be capable of carrying fifteen passengers.[33]

Poor Lippincott: his expedition was to be plagued with difficulties from start to finish. The auto did not arrive in time to make the drive at the end of 1901, but it did arrive in Flagstaff on January 2, 1902. That must have been a light winter, for Lippincott immediately announced that he would make the drive the following day, January 3, 1902. He and his friends, Winfield Hogaboom and Tom Chapman, registered at the Commercial Hotel and finalized their plans and preparations.[34]

Lippincott wisely asked Al Doyle, the man who had built the new road to the Canyon, to be his guide. He showed off the car on the morning of January 3rd by driving it around town, which proved that everything was functioning satisfactorily. He pronounced himself ready and predicted that the party would reach the Grand Canyon in three and one-half hours. He was so confident of this that he did not allow any margin for error, leaving town in the middle of the afternoon.[35] It must have been quite a sight. The car had an open top, so the men were bundled up against the weather. In order to make room for the men and their provisions, a trailer-car had been attached to the vehicle, with two men in each conveyance, and Lippincott at the tiller.

The route to the Canyon had been cryptically described to them by Al Doyle:

> After you get over the rise just outside of town,...you strike down through Fort valley, and bear off to the west, so's not to get too far up onto the foothills while you're getting by the peaks. You hit the new trail there and cross the big wash, and pretty soon you get into the trees. Dry Tanks is about four miles, east of you, and after you pass Sheep Ranch and come up out of the gulch you turn east again, till you get to the clearing. The trail goes right straight into Moodyspan's cabin [Mudersbach's], and then you strike into the trees again until you get to Red mountain. Then you take off across the desert and follow the old sheep trail till you strike the mouth of Red Horse canyon. Just left of the Dog Knobs you come into the cedars again, and keep right through on the old trail till you get to Skinner's cabin. Then you have to bear off down the gulch to the right and follow the gulch. After you strike the old trail back of Red buttes you follow it right in to Berry's.[36]

No wonder they brought Doyle along as a guide.

The run went smoothly until they were just out of town, when they had their first breakdown.[37] They made repairs, then sailed through Fort Valley, where Hogaboom mentioned seeing the old fort. The valley itself, he said, was uninhabited.[38] The delay for repairs had been so long that night was falling. Their ill-advised confidence had been so strong that they had brought no food, only fuel. Doyle advised that they had better put up for the night; so they switched off the boilers and hiked to Mudersbach Cabin, where they found three cowboys who shared their food with them.[39] In the morning they found that their boilers had frozen overnight, so they had to burn gallons of their precious gasoline to thaw them out. Eventually they resumed their journey.[40]

The morning began gloriously, as for ten miles they, "scooted through the forest like sliding down the chutes," before they burst a water gauge. They fixed it after much labor, only to encounter their next problem: they had burned all the gasoline they had brought from Los Angeles and upon switching to the fuel purchased in Flagstaff, they found that it was contaminated and that with it they could only go three miles an hour, belching a plume of black smoke. They finally jettisoned the trailer and all piled into the main car. After another mile, the drive chain broke. By the time they had it mended it was midnight. They were then eighteen miles from the Grandview Hotel, their destination. They ditched the car and started slogging along on foot, a distance that was too much for everyone but Hogaboom. Late the next day Hogaboom straggled into the Grandview, where Pete Berry launched a rescue. He sent out a team of horses and a wagon, picked up the three hikers and —oh, irony!— the horses towed the auto to the Grandview. Next day they made repairs and drove the car to the Bright Angel Hotel, which had a telephone. They placed a call for gasoline to be sent up on the train. Hogaboom, Doyle and Chapman eventually took the train to Williams. They checked in with the editor of the *Williams News*, George Young, a chauvinistic Williams booster, who reported the visit acidly,

A car on the Long Jim Canyon Road, built in 1896 by J. W. Thurber, and used until the late 1920s.

> Just as the *News* went to press last Saturday, three forlorn looking personages rushed into the office and shouted: 'We went to the Grand Canyon on the automobile!' Just at present we cannot recall the names of two of the gentlemen: one was representing the *Los Angeles Herald* and the other some paper in New York. The latter gentleman had written several stanzas of poetry descriptive of the hardships of the trip and promised to send us a copy of the paper contains the article. The third man was Mr. Doyle, of Flagstaff, and they all looked as though they had been traveling with a threshing machine instead of an up to date automobile.[41]

Lippincott, refusing to abandon his mission, waited several days at the Grandview making sure that his car was ready, then drove the Toledo from the Grandview to Flagstaff. While the trip up had been a comedy of errors, taking three days instead of three hours, the return trip showed the potential of auto travel, for it was made in seven hours with only minor difficulties.[42]

In spite of the horrors of the first trip from Flagstaff to the Grand Canyon, even Hogaboom could see that an automobile line would work. He wrote,

> Without doubt, an automobile line will be established next summer between Flagstaff and the canyon. It is the best, and in fact the only route for sightseers. The country is full of natural attractions, and scenery and climate are superb.[43]

Once back in Flagstaff, Lippincott drove the steamer around Flagstaff, giving free rides and touting the future of Grand Canyon travel. He took John G. Verkamp on a demonstration drive up Mars Hill to Lowell Observatory, which so impressed the Flagstaff resident that he determined that he would start an auto stage line. Verkamp went to his home town, Cincinnati, to see about lining up the proper backing.[44] It did not materialize. In 1905, Verkamp founded the famous Verkamp's Curio Store, still a Grand Canyon institution.[45]

Verkamp's plan failed. Nothing more was heard about an auto stage to the Canyon until 1903, when the *Sun* ran a brief item: "An auto line from Flagstaff to Grand Canyon is a talked of possibility of the near future."[46]

No regular auto line from Flagstaff to the Grand Canyon was ever established to replace the Grand Canyon-Flagstaff Stagecoach Line. Instead, the travel situation reverted to the status it had before the line was established: people could take their own vehicles to the Canyon or they could go to an auto livery and rent a car or a car and driver.

In 1907 Fred Lynch took the livery trip in a party that consisted of two cars. The lead car was driven by the owner of the livery, Mr. McLucas (probably a name that was disguised for the purpose of the article), who had "four female school teachers from the Normal" with him. It was McLucas's thirteenth trip that summer. They left town at 6:30 a.m. and drove to the "Cedars," which seems to have been East Cedar Ranch, which was not a stop on the Doyle road, so it seems that the auto livery service was using one of the old stagecoach roads. There was a stash of gasoline at Cedar, and they refueled. From there they followed the old stage road to Moqui, still described as a "water hole." They had many mechanical failures, reminiscent of the Lippincott trip, which caused them to reach Pete Berry's hotel at six p.m. rather than at noon as planned. On the way back the following day the travelers had more misadventures, including equipment failure and the trailing car getting lost. The travelers paid ten dollars per person for their tour. Lynch opined,

> Probably automobiles are the proper caper for some people, but next times, believe me, it'll be the good old horse and wagon for mine.[47]

Given a choice, however, very few people agreed with Lynch. Technical improvements continued to make automobiles faster, safer and more reliable; so that within a few years, no one was going from Flagstaff to the Grand Canyon via horse and wagon. By 1913 the route of choice was a modification of the old Eastern Route on the stage line. Drivers leaving Flagstaff would go north of town on the route of today's Highway 89 until they neared Deadman Flat, when they would veer away to the west, running through the cinder hills until they reached Lockwood Canyon. They would then travel up the canyon, where the old road joined the auto route at Upper Lockwood Tanks, then follow the old stage road up past Moqui and on to the South Rim.[48] After the Grandview Hotel closed, about 1916, auto travel from Flagstaff shifted to the Grand Canyon Village area; so drivers thereafter took different routes. Several roads were developed, eventually resulting in the three routes favored by today's drivers: Highway 64 from Williams, Highway 180 from Flagstaff and Highway 64 from Flagstaff via Cameron.

The appeal of sending an automobile to the Grand Canyon was irresistible to manufacturers. In 1916, the Metz Company sent a driver and photographer out and produced a series of advertising shots

GCM 16412

Endnotes

1. *Coconino Sun,* February 4, 1899.

2. Source unknown. Clipping found in Grand Canyon File, Sharlot Hall Museum, Prescott. The *Williams News* claimed that the story was a hoax in another clipping contained in the same file. The *Flagstaff Gem* published an article on January 12, 1899, stating that the automobiles would be driven down the Bright Angel Trail to a hotel at Indian Garden, an obvious impossibility to anyone familiar with the area.

3. *Coconino Sun,* April 21, 1900.

4. *Flagstaff Gem,* May 17, 1900.

5. *Flagstaff Gem,* July 20, 1900.

6. *Coconino Sun,* July 14, 1900.

7. *Coconino Sun,* July 14, 1900.

8. *Coconino Sun,* July 14, 1900.

9. *Coconino Sun,* July 28, 1900.

10. *Coconino Sun,* August 2, 1900.

11. *Flagstaff Gem,* August 2, 1900 and *Coconino Sun,* August 11, 1900.

12. *Coconino Sun,* August 11, 1900.

13. *Flagstaff Gem,* August 23, 1900.

14. *Flagstaff Gem,* September 6, 1900.

15. *Coconino Sun,* September 8, 1900.

16. *Flagstaff Gem,* June 20, 1900.

17. *Flagstaff Gem,* August 22, 1900.

18. Records of Coconino County, Drawer B (4) Map 3.

19. *Flagstaff Gem,* November 1, 1900.

20. Coconino Sun, November 3, 1900.

21. *Flagstaff Gem,* November 15, 1900.

22. *Coconino Sun,* December 1, 1900 and *Flagstaff Gem,* December 6, 1900.

23. C. A. Higgins. *Grand Cañon of the Colorado.* Santa Fe Railroad. 1901 edition. Insert.

24. *Flagstaff Gem,* February 7, 1901.

25. *Coconino Sun,* April 13, 1901.

26. *Flagstaff Gem,* May 9, 1901.

27. *Coconino Sun,* November 30, 1901.

28. *Coconino Sun,* December 14, 1901.

29. Schullery, Paul, editor. *Grand Canyon, Early Impressions.* Colorado Associated University Press. 1981. p. 59.

30. *Arizona Highways Magazine.* "The Grand Canyon Caper." John Matthews. August 1977. Vol. 53 No. 8:36-41.

31. Lippincott, Oliver. *Glimpses of the Grand Canyon of the Colorado.* Frank S. Thayer Co. Denver. 1900. Schullery op. cit. p. 59.

32. *Coconino Sun,* December 28, 1901.

33. *Coconino Sun,* December 28, 1901.

34. *Flagstaff Gem,* January 2, 1902.

35. *Coconino Sun,* January 4, 1902.

36. Schullery. *op. cit.* p. 60.

37. *Coconino Sun,* February 8, 1902.

38. Schullery, *op. cit.* p. 58.

39. *Coconino Sun,* February 8, 1902.

40. *Ibid.*

41. *Williams News,* January 18, 1902.

42. *Coconino Sun,* February 8, 1902.

43. Schullery. *op. cit.* p. 69.

44. *Coconino Sun,* January 25, 1902.

45. *Coconino Sun,* March 24, 1905.

46. *Coconino Sun,* October 10, 1903.

47. *Out West Magazine.* "An Automobile Trip to the Grand Canyon of Arizona." Fred Lynch. Vol. 26:243-245.

48. *Arizona Good Roads Association Illustrated Road Maps and Tour Book.* Original edition 1913. Reprint. Arizona Highways Magazine. 1987. p. 26.

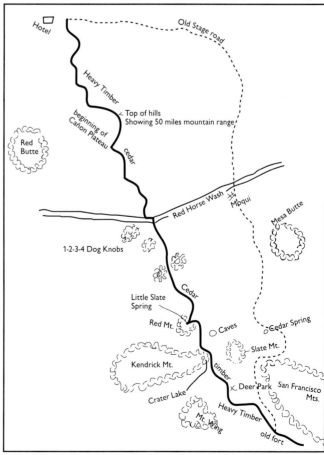

S. E. Faroat's Map, which he filed in support of his Toll Road Certificate, October 30, 1900. The map is sorely lacking in detail, but it does show the stage road, making it abundantly clear that the Faroat-Doyle auto road was different. The route shown by the heavy line here was the road followed by the Lippincott Party on the first auto run from Flagstaff to the Grand Canyon in January 1902. The Grandview Hotel was the end point. The map is computer enhanced, to make Faroat's poorly scrawled labels legible

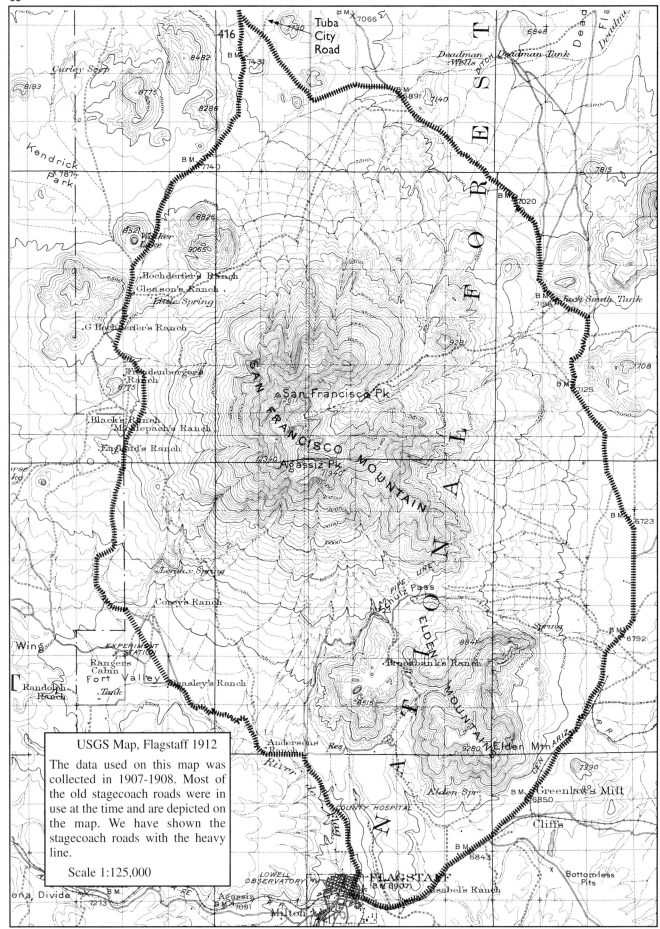

USGS Map, Flagstaff 1912

The data used on this map was collected in 1907-1908. Most of the old stagecoach roads were in use at the time and are depicted on the map. We have shown the stagecoach roads with the heavy line.

Scale 1:125,000

EXPLORATION GUIDE

Exploring the Grand Canyon -
Flagstaff Stagecoach Route & Sites Today
Driving, Biking, Hiking

DRIVING

To follow the stagecoach routes today, drivers must adapt to changes that have occurred in the last one hundred years, as much private property has cut off access to the roads.

Western Route

There are basically three different motor trips:

ALL CARS—EASY TRIP

From Flagstaff around the Hart Prairie Loop. This is an easy scenic drive that can be made in any car except a tail-dragger. Many people take this tour in mid-October to see the changing leaves in the abundant aspen groves found around Hart Prairie. *Time:* 4 hours. *Distance:* 41.35 miles.

HIGH-CLEARANCE VEHICLES

From Flagstaff to Grandview via Lockwood Canyon. This route departs from the old stagecoach road at Tubs Ranch about 35 miles north of Flagstaff and uses the auto road that was developed about 1912, before joining the stagecoach road at Lockwood Tanks. Moderately rough roads make high clearance necessary. *Time:* Most of a day, including sightseeing at the Grand Canyon. *Distance:* 74 miles.

4 X 4S ONLY

From Flagstaff to Grand Canyon via Rabbit Canyon. This closely approximates the true stagecoach road but has some very rough sections. This is for experienced 4-wheelers. *Time:* All day. *Distance:* 76.75 miles.

Eastern Route

There is one decent auto trip over the Eastern Route, but it requires 4-wheel drive. In places, some of the roads are rough, so speeds are slow. *Time*: All day. *Distance*: 80.05 mi. one-way to the Canyon.

BIKING

If you are in *good* condition and are used to the high elevations you will encounter, you may make the whole trip from Flagstaff to the Grand Canyon in one day. Otherwise, make plans for a two-day trip, camping overnight along the way. This means arranging support, and doing a lot of advance preparation. Another option is to do portions of the road. The Western Route is well-known to bikers, but the Eastern Route has been lost in the mists of time. By studying maps and doing field work we have relocated the Eastern Route. *Time*: A long day. *Distance* 77.15 miles.

You will pass through miles of remote and lonely country. Frankly, miles of the ride are rather boring. We strongly recommend that you have company on this trip and do not try it alone.

HIKING

The Arizona Trail follows approximately forty miles of the old stagecoach road. We have read accounts written by those who have hiked the Arizona Trail along the old stagecoach road and believe that hikers are not very well served by anything so far in print. Since we know the area so well, we have bitten off the Arizona Trail in bite-sized chunks. For those who are trying to cover a lot of ground, perhaps hiking the entire trail or very long portions of it at a time, we advise that you prepare yourself properly, offering the following tips:

1. You are traveling through remote country, where you are unlikely to see anyone else. You cannot count on finding help in the event of a problem. Take a companion, cell phone, etc. As the Boy Scouts say, be prepared.

2. Water is very scarce. One of the alarming things we found was that writers are advising hikers that there is water at East Cedar Tank. Not true. The spring there went dry in 1996. You can't count on finding water there, and there is none for miles in the area. Do not count on getting water from the ranch houses, as the occupants are not prepared for this.

3. The rainy season is July, August and the first part of September, and can turn the roads and trails into unpleasant mud bogs. May and June usually have good dry weather but bring out the swarming Juniper Gnats with their most unpleasant bite. Best time is mid-September through October.

4. Most of the country through which you will hike is an active cattle ranching area. Purify all water from stock ponds before drinking, as cattle carry giardia. Set up camp where you won't be trampled in the dark by wandering cows.

5. See our map on page 94 for more details and ideas.

FINDING SITES AT GRAND CANYON

When you follow the old stagecoach route today, you reach the Grand Canyon at a point where Forest Road 310 meets Highway 64, the East Rim Drive. Although the Park Service does not alert the traveler to the historical riches of the area, the place is full of interest. The following sites are all nearby. You could cover all of them in a couple of hours.

1. Hance Camp. See page 95.

2. Old Hance Trail, See page 95.

3. Grandview Hotel Site, See page 96.

4. Grandview Trail, See page 96.

e-mail us for updates: mangum@hexagonpress.com

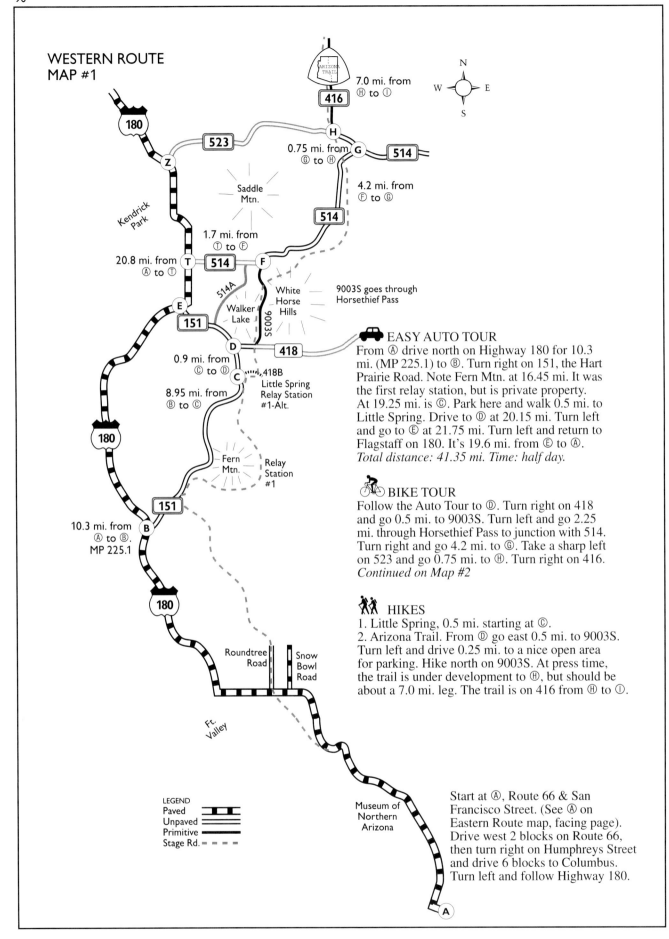

WESTERN ROUTE
MAP #1

180

523

416   7.0 mi. from
Ⓗ to Ⓘ

Z

Ⓗ   0.75 mi. from
Ⓖ to Ⓗ   Ⓖ   514

514   4.2 mi. from
Ⓕ to Ⓖ

Saddle
Mtn.

Kendrick
Park

1.7 mi. from
Ⓣ to Ⓕ

20.8 mi. from   Ⓣ   514   Ⓕ
Ⓐ to Ⓣ

514A   White
Horse
Hills   9003S goes through
Horsethief Pass

Ⓔ
Walker
Lake

151

9003S

Ⓓ   418

0.9 mi. from
Ⓒ to Ⓓ   Ⓒ   418B
Little Spring
Relay Station
#1-Alt.

8.95 mi. from
Ⓑ to Ⓒ

180

Fern
Mtn.   Relay
Station
#1

151

10.3 mi. from   Ⓑ
Ⓐ to Ⓑ.
MP 225.1

180

Roundtree
Road   Snow
Bowl
Road

Ft.
Valley

🚗 EASY AUTO TOUR
From Ⓐ drive north on Highway 180 for 10.3
mi. (MP 225.1) to Ⓑ. Turn right on 151, the Hart
Prairie Road. Note Fern Mtn. at 16.45 mi. It was
the first relay station, but is private property.
At 19.25 mi. is Ⓒ. Park here and walk 0.5 mi. to
Little Spring. Drive to Ⓓ at 20.15 mi. Turn left
and go to Ⓔ at 21.75 mi. Turn left and return to
Flagstaff on 180. It's 19.6 mi. from Ⓔ to Ⓐ.
Total distance: 41.35 mi. Time: half day.

🚴 BIKE TOUR
Follow the Auto Tour to Ⓓ. Turn right on 418
and go 0.5 mi. to 9003S. Turn left and go 2.25
mi. through Horsethief Pass to junction with 514.
Turn right and go 4.2 mi. to Ⓖ. Take a sharp left
on 523 and go 0.75 mi. to Ⓗ. Turn right on 416.
Continued on Map #2

🚶 HIKES
1. Little Spring, 0.5 mi. starting at Ⓒ.
2. Arizona Trail. From Ⓓ go east 0.5 mi. to 9003S.
Turn left and drive 0.25 mi. to a nice open area
for parking. Hike north on 9003S. At press time,
the trail is under development to Ⓗ, but should be
about a 7.0 mi. leg. The trail is on 416 from Ⓗ to Ⓘ.

Museum of
Northern
Arizona

Start at Ⓐ, Route 66 & San
Francisco Street. (See Ⓐ on
Eastern Route map, facing page).
Drive west 2 blocks on Route 66,
then turn right on Humphreys Street
and drive 6 blocks to Columbus.
Turn left and follow Highway 180.

LEGEND
Paved
Unpaved
Primitive
Stage Rd.

Ⓐ

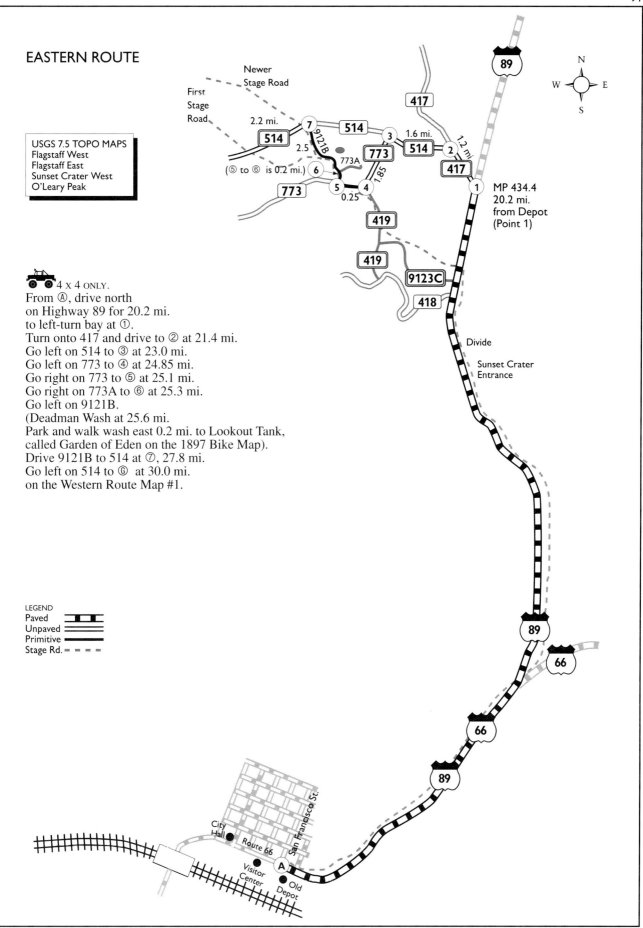

EASTERN ROUTE

USGS 7.5 TOPO MAPS
Flagstaff West
Flagstaff East
Sunset Crater West
O'Leary Peak

4 X 4 ONLY.
From Ⓐ, drive north
on Highway 89 for 20.2 mi.
to left-turn bay at ①.
Turn onto 417 and drive to ② at 21.4 mi.
Go left on 514 to ③ at 23.0 mi.
Go left on 773 to ④ at 24.85 mi.
Go right on 773 to ⑤ at 25.1 mi.
Go right on 773A to ⑥ at 25.3 mi.
Go left on 9121B.
(Deadman Wash at 25.6 mi.
Park and walk wash east 0.2 mi. to Lookout Tank,
called Garden of Eden on the 1897 Bike Map).
Drive 9121B to 514 at ⑦, 27.8 mi.
Go left on 514 to Ⓖ at 30.0 mi.
on the Western Route Map #1.

LEGEND
Paved
Unpaved
Primitive
Stage Rd.

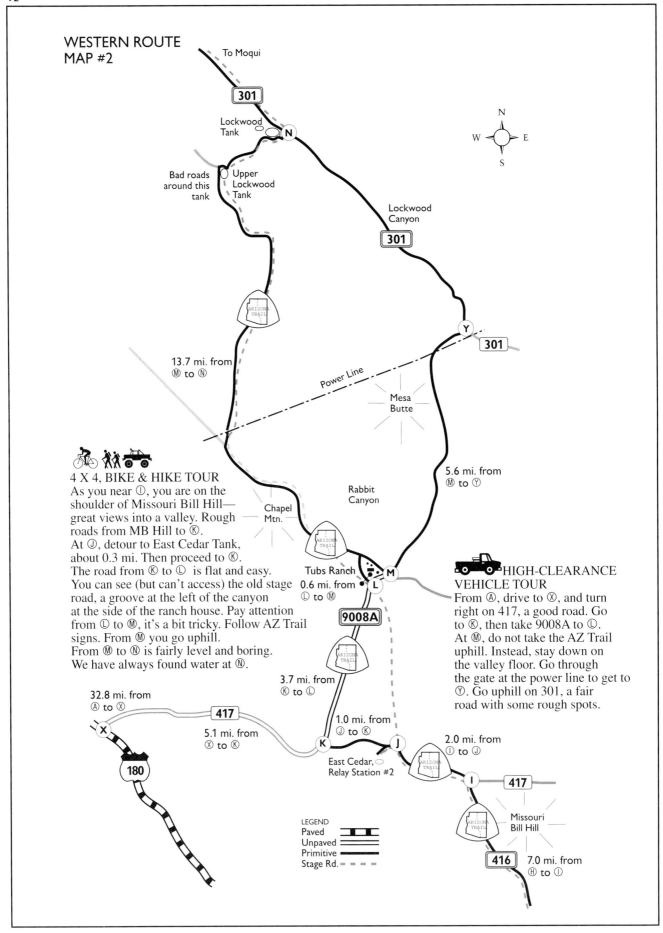

WESTERN ROUTE MAP #2

To Moqui

301

Lockwood Tank

N

Bad roads around this tank

Upper Lockwood Tank

Lockwood Canyon

301

Y

301

13.7 mi. from Ⓜ to Ⓝ

Power Line

Mesa Butte

5.6 mi. from Ⓜ to Ⓨ

Rabbit Canyon

4 X 4, BIKE & HIKE TOUR

As you near Ⓛ, you are on the shoulder of Missouri Bill Hill—great views into a valley. Rough roads from MB Hill to Ⓚ.
At Ⓙ, detour to East Cedar Tank, about 0.3 mi. Then proceed to Ⓚ.
The road from Ⓚ to Ⓛ is flat and easy. You can see (but can't access) the old stage road, a groove at the left of the canyon at the side of the ranch house. Pay attention from Ⓛ to Ⓜ, it's a bit tricky. Follow AZ Trail signs. From Ⓜ you go uphill.
From Ⓜ to Ⓝ is fairly level and boring. We have always found water at Ⓝ.

Chapel Mtn.

Tubs Ranch
0.6 mi. from Ⓛ to Ⓜ

M
L

9008A

HIGH-CLEARANCE VEHICLE TOUR

From Ⓐ, drive to Ⓧ, and turn right on 417, a good road. Go to Ⓚ, then take 9008A to Ⓛ. At Ⓜ, do not take the AZ Trail uphill. Instead, stay down on the valley floor. Go through the gate at the power line to get to Ⓨ. Go uphill on 301, a fair road with some rough spots.

3.7 mi. from Ⓚ to Ⓛ

1.0 mi. from Ⓙ to Ⓚ

32.8 mi. from Ⓐ to Ⓧ

417

X

180

5.1 mi. from Ⓧ to Ⓚ

K   J

2.0 mi. from Ⓘ to Ⓙ

East Cedar, Relay Station #2

I   417

Missouri Bill Hill

416   7.0 mi. from Ⓗ to Ⓘ

LEGEND
Paved
Unpaved
Primitive
Stage Rd.

WESTERN ROUTE MAP #3

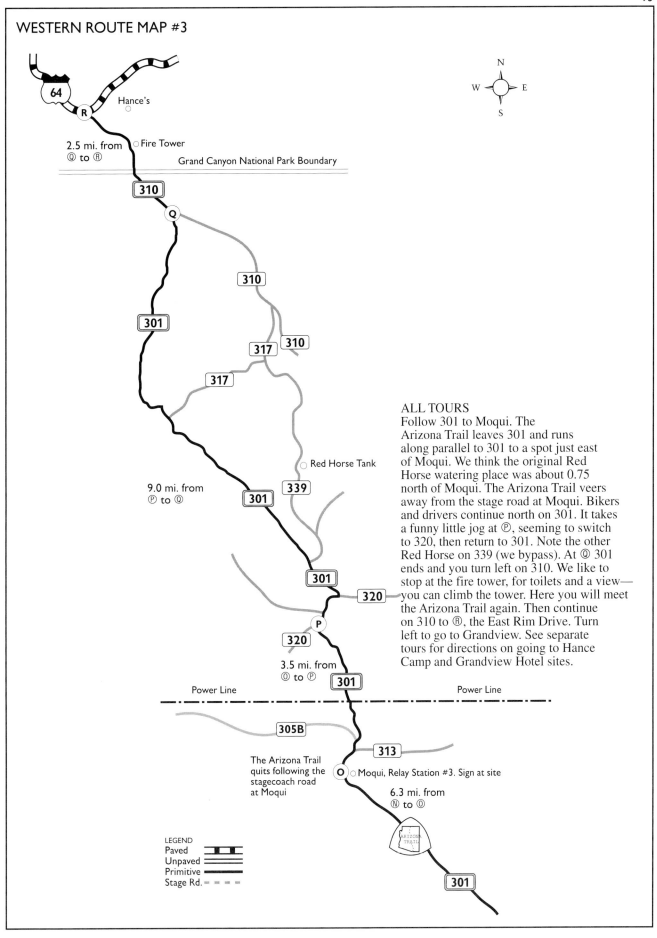

64

Hance's

R

2.5 mi. from
Ⓠ to Ⓡ

Fire Tower

Grand Canyon National Park Boundary

310

Q

310

301

317   310

317

Red Horse Tank

9.0 mi. from
Ⓟ to Ⓠ

339

301

ALL TOURS
Follow 301 to Moqui. The
Arizona Trail leaves 301 and runs
along parallel to 301 to a spot just east
of Moqui. We think the original Red
Horse watering place was about 0.75
north of Moqui. The Arizona Trail veers
away from the stage road at Moqui. Bikers
and drivers continue north on 301. It takes
a funny little jog at Ⓟ, seeming to switch
to 320, then return to 301. Note the other
Red Horse on 339 (we bypass). At Ⓠ 301
ends and you turn left on 310. We like to
stop at the fire tower, for toilets and a view—
you can climb the tower. Here you will meet
the Arizona Trail again. Then continue
on 310 to Ⓡ, the East Rim Drive. Turn
left to go to Grandview. See separate
tours for directions on going to Hance
Camp and Grandview Hotel sites.

301

320

P

320

3.5 mi. from
Ⓞ to Ⓟ

301

Power Line   Power Line

305B

313

The Arizona Trail
quits following the
stagecoach road
at Moqui

O   Moqui, Relay Station #3. Sign at site

6.3 mi. from
Ⓝ to Ⓞ

ARIZONA
TRAIL

301

LEGEND
Paved
Unpaved
Primitive
Stage Rd.

THE ARIZONA TRAIL

MOQUI TO LOCKWOOD TANK

There is a trail marker by the cistern at Moqui. The trail goes E from there, up a little rise. At 0.2 mi. is a trail junction and sign. Turn right (S), sign reads *Forest Boundary 5 mi.* You walk a nice piñon-juniper forest parallel to 301, which you can see to your right. The trail here is easy to follow. At 1.66 mi. the trail crosses 301. Trail dim and uncertain here. Don't walk down the road. Go across, staying on the line of the footpath. In about 100 yards you will find the trail again, marked by several poles and rocks. From here, the trail moves parallel to the road, west of it; so far away from the road you can seldom see it.

At 4.75 mi. you swing back toward the road and enter an open field. The trail moves across the field to the point where the Kaibab Forest boundary fence meets 301 at a cattle guard at 5.2 miles. This is not a good place to camp, as there is no water.

From the cattle guard walk down 301 for 1.6 miles to Lockwood Tank, a dependable water source, but treat the water before you drink it. If camping, go up on a high point so cows won't step on you. *Distance: 6.8 mi.*

O Moqui Stage Station

6.8 mi.

Lockwood **N**
Tank

LOCKWOOD TANK TO TUBS RANCH

Walk through the second high-post gate in the fence into a corral. The floor is beaten bare by the hooves of cattle, but you will see tire tracks running SW, showing the way. Beyond the corrals you'll see the road that you walk. It goes along a shallow limestone canyon to emerge into a plain. It's sagebrush, piñon and juniper country, with no shade. At 1.9 mi. you reach Upper Lockwood Tank—usually contains water. The road curves around its base; very rough for vehicles here. You round the tank and head south, going up a series of rocky terraces. From 3.75 mi. hikers enjoy views of the San Francisco Peaks and volcanic field full of cones and craters. You'll reach Little Buckhorn Tank—looks like a railroad water car lying on its side—at 6.0 mi.

At 8.2 mi. you come to a big power line. Confusing here. Look carefully for trail markers. Go to the SE at the line, going uphill. Do not go down into the flat toward the ponds.

Beyond the power line there are few landmarks. There is a ranch gate at 12.2 mi. From here you are only about 1.0 mi. from the edge of a mesa. Fine views. From the rim, you will come down to Ⓜ to finish the trail segment. Ⓜ is not a good place to camp. If camping, stay up on the mesa. It will be a dry camp—no water. *Distance: 13.7 mi.*

13.7 mi.

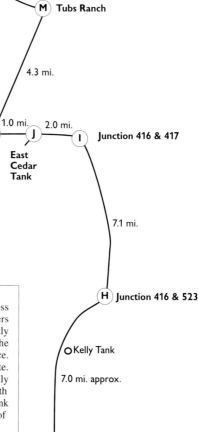

TUBS RANCH TO EAST CEDAR TANK

This leg of the Arizona Trail is easy, but not very interesting, as it proceeds along the flat valley floor from one side of the valley to the other. You walk along road 9008A from M to K, then turn east on road 417. Look for the side-road up to East Cedar Tank. It is unmarked, but easy to spot, as there is no other road in that area. The tank is up on a bench from which there are great views. This is a good camping spot, but there is no water. *Total: 5.6 mi.*

M Tubs Ranch

4.3 mi.

Cedar Ranch **K** 1.0 mi. **J** 2.0 mi. **I** Junction 416 & 417

East
Cedar
Tank

EAST CEDAR TANK TO JUNCTION OF 416 & 523

From E. Cedar Tank, go downhill, turn right and go through the gate. Stay on 417 to its junction with 416 at 2.25 mi., where you turn right (S). You will now climb 600 feet to the side of Missouri Bill Hill at 4.2 mi. Great views to the north. This is the highest point, and you will now head downhill, walking on 416. AZ Trail signs mark the way. This is a fairly scenic stretch and at places at the side of the road you can see the old stagecoach road as a shallow depression. As you near the end you re-enter Ponderosa pine habitat. No water. *Distance: 9.4 mi.*

7.1 mi.

JUNCTION OF 416 & 523 TO 418

Hike from the junction of 416 and 523 south, across country. At 0.2 mi. you come to a jeep road; the trail veers away from it to your left (E) winding over rolling but mostly level ground, heading south. You're on the route of the stagecoach but can't see ruts, lines of rocks or other evidence. At 0.8 mi. the trail rejoins the jeep path just before a gate.

Go through the gate, turn right (W) and hike 514 to Kelly Tank. The forest here was burned in April 1996. To the south are glimpses of the San Francisco Peaks. You reach Kelly Tank (unreliable water) at 3.0 mi. At press time, the route south of Kelly Tank has not been determined, except that it will go through Horsethief Pass (Map #1). *Distance: 7.0 mi.*

H Junction 416 & 523

○ Kelly Tank

7.0 mi. approx.

D 418

Hance Camp & Lookout Point

From the Junction of FR 310 and Highway 64, the East Rim Drive, turn right (E) and go 1.25 miles (MP 253.7) to the Buggeln Picnic Area. Pull left into the picnic area and park. Walk NE on the East Rim Drive for 0.3 miles, where you will find MP 254. Continue walking 150 paces downhill on the paved road. You will see that the road comes very close to the Canyon's edge here, at a kind of notch. At this point, turn to your right and hike south, down off the road into a valley, bearing slightly to the right as you descend. You will see a leveled placed where stones outline the Buggeln Hotel building site. Buggeln built his hotel in 1907 just east of the Hance Camp, where the stage line's tents were located. All buildings at the site were removed in 1957.

After exploring the area, you will want to go to the place where the stagecoach travelers got their first view of the Grand Canyon. Walk uphill and cross the road, to the narrow point or notch mentioned above. Turn to the right (E) a bit and you will see a trail going uphill to an exposed white rock outcrop. The tip of this outcrop was Lookout or Observation Point. The foot trail to the top is still plainly visible and easy to follow. It is a short walk.

The views from the point are spectacular.

GPS Readings UTM
Hance Camp—0414358 3982170
Observation Point—0414561 3982211

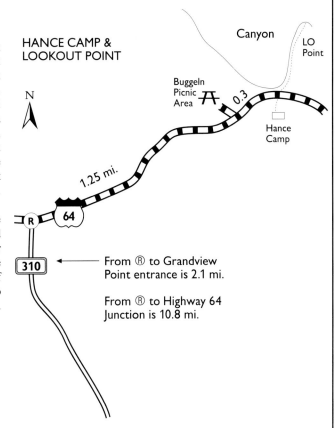

From ⓡ to Grandview Point entrance is 2.1 mi.

From ⓡ to Highway 64 Junction is 10.8 mi.

Old Hance Trailhead & Hance's New Cabin

From the Buggeln Picnic Area (see above), walk east along the road for 0.9 miles. Here you will find the site of a viewpoint that has been closed. There is a line of big rocks and a crushed gravel apron from the days when it was a viewpoint for motorists, but a high curb has been built between the parking area and the road to prevent entry. It was never a big area, just about one car-length deep.

1. *Trailhead.* The trailhead was right at the parking place, though we did not find any cairns, blazes or other markers. If you walk out on the rim to the east, you can look back and see that there is only one way the trail could have come down, which is an alluvial slide in a cliff-gap. The trailhead would have been about a half-mile on a direct line from Hance's Camp. It is impassable and dangerous. Don't try to hike it.
GPS Reading UTM 0415138 3982455.

2. *Cabin site.* From the old viewpoint, walk west a few yards to a point where there is a shelf of fairly level land. The cabin was on this shelf, very close to the rim. We found a pile of stones, the remains of the chimney. If one looks closely, there are other materials, such as nails, broken glass, etc. Also, behind the cabin are a lot of rusted cans. The cabin was surprisingly close to the rim, and this would have exposed it to some harsh winds. Maybe the view was worth it.
GPS Reading UTM 0415015 3982384.

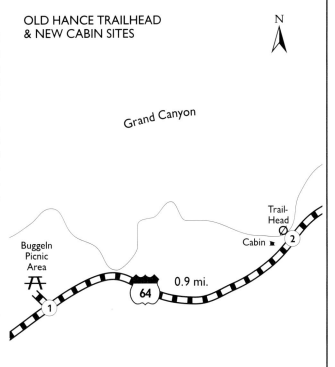

Grandview Hotel Location

From the junction of FR 310 and the East Rim Drive, turn left and drive 1.5 miles to MP 251. There, on the right side of the road, you will see a parking area. Pull over and park. At the southeast end of the parking area is an old road with a barrier at its entrance and a CLOSED ROAD sign. Hike this road about 0.5 miles to the site of the Hotel.

There is not much to see at the old hotel site, but you can get a feel for how things were in the old days. Trees have grown up in what used to be a clearing, changing the appearance. All the buildings have been torn down, but if you look carefully, you will see some stones on the ground outlining old structures, and you will find lots of broken glass, nails, etc. On the far (east) side of the hotel site are a series of ponds, known at the Hearst Tanks, in the bottom of a ravine that runs into the Canyon. These ponds mark the extent of the hotel property: don't go past them.

GPS Reading UTM 0411275 3982078.

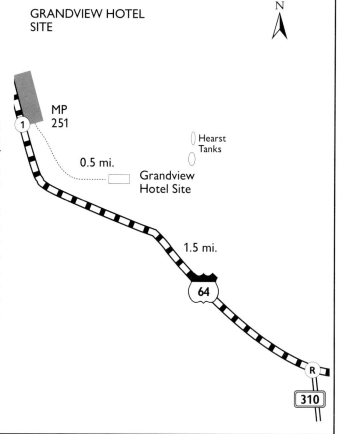

GRANDVIEW HOTEL SITE

Original Grandview Trail

Drive up the Grandview Point entrance road for 0.25 mi. There is no place to park at this point but make a note of it so you can return here on foot. The old trailhead is due east [from True North] 0.14 miles from this point. Drive on to Grandview Point, loop around and park in the upper parking lot [farthest away from the rim], then backtrack on foot 0.35 miles to return to the starting point.

The trailhead area is in a cove, where we found a cairn marking the spot. Side trails take the hiker over to a large bare white rock, which can be easily climbed, providing a superb viewpoint for photographs. The trail itself is typical of the early trails, reminding us of the Old Hance Trail. It follows an alluvial slide, making a tight corkscrew to get down off the highest levels. We followed it for perhaps 0.1 mile, reaching a place where a washout has turned a downgrade into a chute. Here we turned back.

NOTE: We caution readers that this trail has not been used for many years and has received no maintenance. Plants have grown up in the trail and nearby, so it is necessary to dodge bushes and branches. The footing is rather slippery due to small broken stones everywhere. We rate the trail as dangerous and advise that no one should try to hike it. Do as we did if you want to hike: just going down the very first bit of the trail in order to get a sense of its design, and then come back up to safety.

The GPS reading (error factor of about 60 feet): UTM 04 10 928 39 83 393

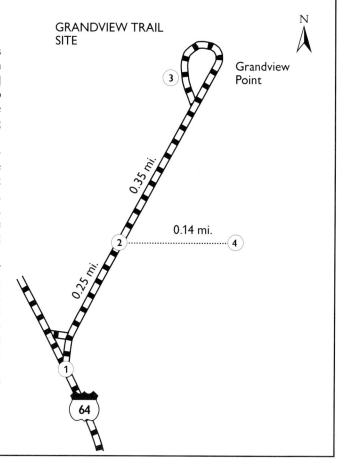

GRANDVIEW TRAIL SITE

Bibliography

Books

Anderson, Michael F. *Living at the Edge.* Grand Canyon Association. Grand Canyon, Arizona. 1998.

Anonymous. *America Her Grandeur and Her Beauty.* Union Book & Publishing Company. Chicago, New York. ca. 1901.

Anonymous. *Arizona.* Hastings House. New York. 1940.

Ayer, E. E. *Reminiscences.* Unpublished manuscript. Bancroft Library.

Baedeker, Karl. *United States.* 1893 and 1899 editions.

Bicknell, P. C. *Guide Book of the Grand Canyon of Arizona.* Printed by George U. Young. 1901.

Billingsley, George H.; Spamer, Earle E.; Menkes, Dove. *Quest for the Pillar of Gold.* Grand Canyon Association. Grand Canyon, Arizona. 1997.

Cleeland, Teri. "To Hull and Back" article in *People and Places of the Old Kaibab.* USDA Forest Service Southwest Region, Report #10. September 1990.

Colton, Harold S. and Baxter, Frank C. *Days on the Painted Desert and In The San Francisco Mountains.* Coyote Range. Flagstaff. 1927.

Corle, Edwin. *Listen, Bright Angel.* Duell, Sloan and Pearce. New York. 1946.

D'Emilio, Sandra and Campbell, Suzan. *The Art & Artists of the Santa Fe Railway.* Peregrine Smith Books. Salt Lake City. 1991.

Dysart, Zella. *Summer Sojourn to the Grand Canyon, the 1898 Diary of Zella Dysart,* edited by Mona L. McCroskey. HollyBear Press, Prescott, AZ. 1996.

Evans, Edna. *Tales from the Grand Canyon.* Northland Press. Flagstaff. 1985.

Farquhar, Francis P. *Books of the Colorado River & the Grand Canyon.* W. M. Morrison Books. Austin, Texas. 1991.

Finck, Henry Theophilus. *The Pacific Coast Scenic Tour: from Southern California to Alaska, the Canadian Pacific Railway, Yellowstone Park and the Grand Canon.* Charles Scribner's Sons. New York. 1891.

Flagstaff Symphony Guild. *Flagstaff: 1876-1976, A Random Collection of Antique Photographs & Writings.* Flagstaff. 1976.

Fuchs, James R. *A History of Williams, Arizona.* University of Arizona. Tucson. 1953.

Gerber, Rudy J. *Grand Canyon Railroad.* Primer Publishers. Phoenix. 1990.

Good, John. *Copper—A Guide to Grandview Trail and Horseshoe Mesa.* Grand Canyon Natural History Association. Grand Canyon. 1985.

Greever, William S. *Arid Domain.* Stanford University Press. 1954.

Hall, Sharlot. *Sharlot Herself, Selected Writings.* Sharlot Hall Museum Press. Prescott, AZ. 1992.

Hegemann, Elizabeth. *Navaho Trading Days.* University of New Mexico Press. Albuquerque. 1963.

Higgins, C. A. *Grand Cañon of the Colorado River Arizona* Santa Fe Railroad, Chicago 1893 and subsequent editions.

Higgins, C. A. *Titan of Chasms.* Santa Fe Railroad. Chicago. 1908 and 1911

Hochderffer, George. *Flagstaff Whoa.* Museum of Northern Arizona. Flagstaff. 1965.

Holmes, Burton. *Travelogues,* 1898. The McClure Co. New York. 1908.

Hughes, J. Donald. *In the House of Stone and Light.* Grand Canyon Natural History Association. 1978.

James, George Wharton. *In and Around the Grand Canyon.* Little Brown Company. New York. 1900.

James, George Wharton. *The Grand Canyon of Arizona; How to See It.* Little, Brown, and Company. Boston. Also Fred Harvey. Kansas City. 1910.

Kinsey, Joni Louise. *The Majesty of the Grand Canyon, 150 Years in Art.* First Glance Books. Cobb, California. 1998.

Lippincott, Oliver. *Glimpses of the Grand Canyon of the Colorado.* Frank S. Thayer Co. Denver. ca. 1900.

Lockwood, Frank C. *Arizona Characters.* Los Angeles Times-Mirror Press. 1928.

Lockwood, Frank C. *The Life of Edward E. Ayer.* A. C. McClurg & Co. Chicago. 1929.

Lummis, Charles F. *Some Strange Corners of Our Country.* University of Arizona Press. Tucson. 1989. Reprint of 1892 book.

Manns, Timothy. *A Guide to Grand Canyon Village Historic District.* Grand Canyon Natural History Association. Undated.

Marshall, R. B. *Results of Spirit Leveling in Arizona, 1899 to 1909, Inclusive.* Government Printing Office. Washington. 1911.

Marshall, R. B. *Results of Spirit Leveling in Arizona, 1899 to 1915, Inclusive.* Government Printing Office. Washington. 1915.

McCutcheon, John T. *Doing the Grand Canyon.* Fred Harvey. Chicago. 1909.

Moran, Thomas. *Home Thoughts from Afar, Letters of Thomas Moran to Mary Nimmo Moran.* East Hampton Free Library. East Hampton, NY. 1967.

Munk, Joseph A. *Arizona Sketches.* Grafton Press. New York. 1905.

McClintock, James H. *Arizona.* S. J. Clarke Publishing Co. Chicago. 1916.

Olberding, Susan Deaver. *A History of Fort Valley, Arizona, and Its Forest Experiment Station 1850 to 1992.* Master's Thesis. Northern Arizona University. 1993.

Pattee, C. R. *Land of Sunshine.* Reprint of 1897 article. Northern Arizona Pioneers' Historical Society. Flagstaff. 1975.

Peabody, H. G. *Glimpses of the Grand Canyon of Arizona.* Fred Harvey. Kansas City. 1900.

Richmond, Al. *Rails to the Rim.* Grand Canyon Railway. Flagstaff. 1994.

Santa Fe Railway Company. *Grand Cañon of the Colorado River in Arizona.* June 1, 1897.

Santa Fe Railway Company. *Grand Canyon Outings.* 1915.

Saunders, Charles Francis. *Finding the Worthwhile in the Southwest.* Robert M. McBride & Co. New York. 1918. Revised edition, 1937.

Schullery, Paul, editor. *The Grand Canyon, Early Impressions.* Colorado Associated University Press. 1981.

Seton, Grace Gallatin. *Nimrod's Wife.* Archibald, Constable & Co. London. 1907.

Shock, Donald Paul. *The History of Flagstaff.* Thesis, Northern Arizona University. 1952.

Sloan, Richard E. *Memories of an Arizona Judge.* Stanford University Press. Stanford. 1932.

Smalley, George H. *My Adventures in Arizona.* Arizona Pioneers' Historical Society. Tucson. 1966.

Smith, Dama Margaret. *I Married a Ranger.* Stanford University Press. 1922.

Steele, J. W. *Guide to the Pacific Coast.* Rand, McNally & Co. New York. 1891.

Sutphen, Debra. Master's Thesis, Northern Arizona University. 1991. *Grandview, Hermit, and South Kaibab Trails: Linking the Past, Present and Future at the Grand Canyon of the Colorado, 1890-1990.*

Stoddard, John L. *Stoddard's Lectures.* Vol. 10. Balch Brothers. Boston. 1898.

Theobald, John and Lillian. *Arizona Territory Post Offices & Postmasters.* Arizona Historical Foundation. Phoenix. 1961.

Tinker, George H. *Northern Arizona in 1887.* Arthur H. Clark Company, Glendale, CA. 1969.

Staff of Kaibab National Forest. *Visitors Guide Kaibab National*

Forest. Southwest Natural and Cultural Heritage Association. Albuquerque. 1990.

Van Dyke, John C. *The Grand Canyon of the Colorado.* Reissued. University of Utah Press. Salt Lake City. 1992. [Original issue 1920].

Verkamp, Margaret M. *History of Grand Canyon National Park.* Grand Canyon Pioneers Society. Flagstaff. 1993.

Way, Thomas E. *Destination Grand Canyon.* Golden West Publishers. Phoenix. 1990.

Weigle, Marta and Babcock, Barbara A. *The Great Southwest of the Fred Harvey Company and the Santa Fe Railway.* The Heard Museum. Phoenix. 1996.

Woods, G. K. *Personal Impressions of the Grand Canyon of the Colorado.* The Whitaker and Ray Company. San Francisco. 1899.

Magazines

Arizona Highways. June 1949. Vol. 25, No. 6. "John Hance, Guide, Trail Builder, Miner and Windjammer of the Grand Canyon." Lon Garrison.

Arizona Highways. May 1957. "The Trailblazers of Grand Canyon." Charles F. Parker. pp. 29-30

Arizona Highways. August, 1977. Vol. 53 No. 8 pp. 36-41. "The Grand Canyon Caper." John Matthews.

Arizona and the West. Spring 1978 pp. 41-64 and Summer 1978 pp. 155-172. "Ralph H. Cameron and the Grand Canyon." Douglas H. Strong.

Atlantic Monthly. December 1899. pp. 816-21. "The Grand Canyon of the Colorado." Harriet Monroe.

Cañon Journal. Fall/Winter 1995. Vol. 1, No. 2. "When Roads Were Ruts and the Stagecoach Ruled." Michael F. Anderson.

Catholic World. December 1899. "The Grand Canyon of the Colorado." Anonymous.

Century. November 1902. "The Grand Cañon of the Colorado." John Muir. pp. 107-116.

Desert, January, 1975, pp. 32-35. "Grand Canyon Stage Line". Russell Wahmann.

Grand Canyon Guide. Vol. II, No. 8. July 2-15, 1978. "The Flagstaff to Grand Canyon Stage." Charles B. Wahler.

Harper's New Monthly Magazine. No. 579. August 1898. pp. 377-392. "Under the Spell of the Grand Cañon." T. Mitchell Prudden.

Independent. March 23, 1899. p. 824. "The Grand Cañon of the Colorado." Ralph S. Tarr.

Journal of Arizona History. Vol. 11, No. 1. Spring 1970. "Motoring in Arizona in 1914." Edith S. Kitt. pp. 32-65.

Journal of Arizona History. Vol. 17, No. 1, Spring, 1976. "Railroad at the Rim, The Origin and Growth of Grand Canyon Village." Gordon Chappell.

Journal of Arizona History. Vol. 32, No. 2, Summer, 1991. "Too Hard a Nut to Crack, Peter D. Berry and the Battle for Free Enterprise at the Grand Canyon, 1890-1914." Debra Sutphen.

Land of Sunshine. September 1895. "The Greatest Thing in the World." Charles Lummis.

Land of Sunshine. August 1898. "Into the Grand Canyon." Charles Lummis.

Land of Sunshine. June 1900. "To the Cañon By Rail." C. A. M.

Leslie's Popular Monthly, June 1896. "In the Grand Cañon of the Colorado." Edith Sessions Tupper. pp. 611-677-684.

Mountain Living. June 1986. "Grand Days of the Grandview." June O'Neill King.

Nation. September 7, 1893. "From Flagstaff to the Grand Cañon," pp. 169-170 and "The Most Sublime of Earthly Spectacles," September 14, 1893 pp. 187-188. Henry T. Finck.

Northlander. January 25, 1979. "Northland Back Pages: Grand Canyon by Stage Coach." Cathy Viele.

Out West. Vol. 26:243-245. "An Automobile Trip to the Grand Canyon of Arizona." Fred Lynch.

Scientific American. June 18, 1892 and August 6, 1892. "The Grand Canyon of the Colorado." Horace C. Hovey.

Southwest Illustrated Magazine. October 1895. "The Grand Canyon of the Colorado." G. A. Neeff.

Newspapers

Arizona Champion, Flagstaff, Arizona. Various dates.
Coconino Sun, Flagstaff, Arizona. Various dates.
Gem. Flagstaff, Arizona. Various dates.
Sun-Democrat, Flagstaff, Arizona. Various dates.
Northlander, Flagstaff, January 25, 1979.
Prescott Journal-Miner, Prescott, Arizona. Various dates.
Williams News. Williams, Arizona. Various dates.

Miscellaneous

Arizona Statutes of 1887.
Berry, P. D. file. Grand Canyon Museum Archives. Grand Canyon, Arizona.
Buggeln, Martin, file. Grand Canyon Museum Archives. Grand Canyon, Arizona.
Cameron, Bert, Interview. June 21, 1939. Grand Canyon Park Service Library.
Diary of Grand Canyon Trip in 1898 by Sidney B. Foote. Unpublished paper. Museum of Northern Arizona. MS 196.
Dillman, Albert A. Interview. July 21, 1977. Museum of Northern Arizona. MS 259.
Flagstaff to Grand Canyon Stage Route. Unpublished paper. Trail Feasibility Study. Prepared for Coconino National Forest in 1977 by Jana Shaw and Charles B. Wahler.
Grandview file. Grand Canyon Museum Archives. Grand Canyon, Arizona.
Hearst, W. R. file. Grand Canyon Museum Archives. Grand Canyon, Arizona.
Historical Resources of the Kaibab National Forest. Elizabeth Coker. 1978.
Land Ownership Record. United States Department of the Interior. National Park Service. Grand Canyon. Reference to Deed No. 29.
Map of the Grand Canyon Road 1894. Records of Coconino County, Arizona. File 1 Map 13, Recorder's Office. Flagstaff.
Records of Coconino County, Arizona
Register, Bright Angel Hotel. Museum of Northern Arizona. MS 25.1.
Wilson Collection—MS 162. Special Collections. Northern Arizona University.
Metzger Collection, NAU Special Collections MS 242.
Sharlot Hall Museum *Grand Canyon* File. Prescott, Arizona.

Abbreviations

AHS-PM—Arizona Historical Society-Pioneers' Museum, Flagstaff.
GCM— Grand Canyon Museum Archives. Grand Canyon.
MNA—Museum of Northern Arizona Photo Archives. Flagstaff.
NAU—Cline Library Special Collections. Flagstaff.